For Nina, my darling,

May your awareness
of your precious, eternal,
Divine self expand and
delight you.

I love you
from the bottom
of my ♡ . . . .

B.

All That You Are

by Mary

 DEVORSS *Publications*

ISBN: 0-87516-055-7

Fourteenth Printing, 1995

DeVorss & Company, Publisher
P.O. Box 550
Marina del Rey, CA 90294

Printed in the United States of America

FOREWORD

Somewhere, in the great pool of knowledge which lies in eternity, are the answers to all of the things the human heart so longs to learn, and sometimes the human mind awakens to seeking.

It is my greatest and my deepest desire to be of service in any manner possible to me as a human being, to express my deepest self in the world of mortals that I may perhaps help someone to find his way again if he has become lost, or to help someone find his way for the first time in his present life.

I do not care in which direction I am sent, as long as it is the will of my Creator and as long as I may be of service. This is my only purpose in existing, my only goal in life as well as in death.

If it is my destiny to be a channel for any of the knowledge which will contribute to the awareness of man, then I am humbly and deeply grateful.

—Mary

TABLE OF CONTENTS

YOU

The only solution to the mysteries of man's existence and of his everyday toiling toward a goal he does not understand is to seek the inner self.

Here the answers are waiting to every question concerning eternity, concerning material life, concerning all phases of creation. All things come from the same Source; therefore, all answers are available to everyone. It is simply a matter of awakening awareness, of developing the dormant consciousness.

What do you want most? Do you believe that material possessions make you happier than any other accomplishment in your life? Or have you reached a point of realizing that happiness is not concerned at all with what you possess materially, but is a fountain which bubbles from within and expresses upon the surface in contentment, laughter, a feeling of joy and good will toward the rest of the world?

If you are ready to seek within, to find your true self, to learn to express it so you may go on to greater awarenesses and greater happinesses, then prepare to listen.

Somewhere in your being is a longing, or you would not have found an interest in picking up a book to read. Somewhere within you lies a loneliness, a desire to feel a oneness with that which created you, that which you call God.

You are not a lost unit in the great, great spaces of endlessness which are creation. You are, it is true, but one infinitesimal part and yet you are as important as the largest part of that creation.

11

This is the first lesson to become aware of and to accept; that you are no less than and no more than anything which exists. Not the birds, not the trees, not your fellow man; not a rock or a grain of sand or a speck of dust. Not the sun or the moon, not the stars, not the sea itself. You are not more than any of these, and you are not less.

When you honestly strive to express what is within you as an individual, in honesty and goodwill toward all things, you are fulfilling your destiny and you are expressing in importance equal to those who are public figures, who perform great deeds for the world, and even for those who are knowing beyond your imagination.

Learn to accept that all men are equally important in the eyes of God. If your skin is white, it does not make you a superior being to the man who is black. If your faith is beneath the roof of a great church, it does not make you more virtuous than the man who worships in an opening among the trees. If your material possessions or importance are very highly regarded by your fellow beings, it does not make you more important than the man whose food comes to him in minute quantities, perhaps with many days' interval between his meals.

You are nothing and you have nothing which can make you more imprtant than anyone else; but likewise, nothing and no one else has anything which would make you less important.

You have the right to express yourself as you are, not as the mold of society would present you; not as your living habits and environment have formed you upon the surface, but as that deep one within the core of you which makes you unique.

Just as there are no two snowflakes alike, there are no two human beings identical. You are in a class by yourself. You are something special. All things of creation are special, and if you should drop from sight there would be a gap left in the great circle of creation because your place is reserved for you, and no other can replace you.

Have respect for yourself, because you are a unit of that great Creator which made all things to be. Care for yourself, not in the egotistical way of a human being but in the deep and understanding concern for any part of God.

You are not alone at any moment, because you are a part of creation and yet you stand alone in your search for understanding because no one can show you the exact steps to take and no one can take them for you. Your way can be lighted by the wisdom of those who have reached an understanding, but you cannot be pushed, you cannot be pulled. You can only be encouraged.

If you believe that you are not endowed by the physical beauty others sometimes possess and you are resentful, or you believe you are inferior for this reason, please remember that there were many varieties of everything created, and this includes man. That which is considered beautiful in one country would be considered ugly in another. That which is considered good taste in one country is considered poor taste in another. And so it goes with all phases of the material plane.

You are you. Your features are your own. They do not belong to anyone else, and they are just right for you. If others scoff at you for some seeming physical defect, in time you can learn that it is ignorance, and if you will note, those who scoff are without perfection themselves.

One who has everything has no need to scoff, to criticize, or to condemn. It is for you to understand that you have all the attributes of the greatest person who ever lived and all the potential weaknesses of the least person who ever lived. It is up to you and you alone to find the balance between the two so you may express your self as you were intended to express.

You need not feel that you are excluded from some superior or highly favored circle of individuals who have the inside key or track with God. He does not have favorites. This is one fact which is very difficult for many individuals to accept, because they like to believe that if they deny themselves enough and practice their own particular beliefs enough, they will reach an exalted state beyond that of the rest of their fellow beings.

This simply is not so. God's love is impartial and it is boundless. There are no measuring sticks attached to his love, but only to the so-called love of the human being. The Creator loves equally the murderer, the minister; the financier and the pauper. He does not make any difference between them, and the degree of his love varies only in the ability of the individual to accept it, for it is felt in proportion to the love a being is able to return.

Because God created all things, he is impartial to all of his beings so you need not feel you are neglected, ignored and unloved. You are as close to the heart of God as anyone who has walked the earth. You need only to learn to express the God within you to become fully aware of this fact.

You have been less in your surface expression than what you truly are in your being. If you wish to find your self, you may begin at once by practicing the awareness that you are where you are because you were created for that place. You are not a misfit, you are not a mistake. You are just right.

You have abilities which are yours. They are as good as the abilities of anyone else. You need not try to assume talents you do not have, because your talents are as good as any which belong to someone else.

Learn to express your self as an individual, as *you*. You are a fascinating person. You have wisdom to impart. It is there within you. You have only to gain the habit of expressing.

You need not change your religion to gain this understanding. You will probably broaden it a little, but you need not change it. You need not change your social position. You need not sacrifice anything except the human habit of thinking fearful thoughts. The only thing you must give up eventually, if not immediately, is fear, which includes doubt, self-criticism, worry, envy, resentment—human emotions, surface emotions. The only feeling within you, and deep within you, is love, and this you will learn as you truly and sincerely seek to know your self.

Become aware that you have a place in creation and if you are tempted to feel important beyond others, remember all others too have a special place which you cannot usurp, which you cannot acquire.

Have faith that nothing can stand in the way of your search for understanding. When it is sincere and humble, it is a God-power put into action, and this is invincible.

You have begun your search for the greatest goal of the material plane—happiness. And it will be yours in greater and greater measure as you understand more about yourself and as you express more that which you were intended to be.

Now, take a deep breath, close your eyes, and let the awareness of creation enter you, in all its throbbing beauty and splendor.

RELAXATION

Throughout the universe there runs a great magnetic current. This is the force of God, his hand moving the parts of his creation about, his strength being applied to any action.

If you are seeking an end to your loneliness, you will find the means by using the current. If you are seeking an outlet for your desire to express your abilities, by learning to use the magnetic force properly you will accomplish this goal. If you would travel and see the wonders of the world but you are hampered by financial lack, seek the current, learn to use it, and you can go wherever you wish for as long as you wish.

There is no limit to what you may accomplish through the use of the magnetic force, for it is this force which created all of the world you see about you, all of the animals, all of the plants, all of the human beings. This force created the sky and it created the seas. Because this is God, it has created all things, and it *can* create anything. Through proper use of this force, through you as a material individual, there is also no limit to what may be done with it.

It is true that a mountain can be moved through faith, because faith is the practical application of the magnetic force to any situation, and you are capable of applying this force, because your real self is charged with it, moving through it, one with it.

You may not have heard of the magnetic current before, or if you have, you may have believed it was something far beyond your particular reach. The great ones who have walked the earth have expressed through this force. They came to your planet to show you the way, that you might accomplish the same things they did, learning through their examples.

Jesus healed those who were ill through applying the force, and because the individuals who sought for healing were ready to accept this magnetism, they were healed. Buddha taught that through using the current a man could become so peaceful within himself nothing of the earth could touch him again, and this is truth. Confucius taught that by using the God-force man would no longer say unkind words to his neighbor, or perform unkind deeds upon him. Name any master teacher who has been upon the planet Earth and you will find that each one has, in his own way, expressed the existence of the magnetic current. It is God in tangible action.

The scientists of today have at last "discovered" this current. They will find it can accomplish anything to which they apply it. It will pass any test they wish to give it. And the master teachers who came long before gave proofs of the existence of such a force. Their teachings were scorned at the time, then as the years passed and they were gone, their knowledge was twisted until it could not possibly be understood by the unknowing, and these were the ones the great beings came to contact in the first place.

If you will have patience and perserverance, you will learn how to use the magnetic force in every part of your material existence. This does not refer only to your inner being, although all things must begin from within and be expressed upon the outside if they are to come to a successful conclusion.

RELAXATION

There must be a place of beginning for all things in the material dimension, and this applies to the awareness of and use of the great magnetic current of God. If you would open to the force, begin your opening with a simple exercise.

Find a spot where you can be alone each day. It may be for only a few minutes or it may be for as long as two or three hours. It does not matter, because time is only important to the physical plane of existence. It has no importance whatsoever beyond that, because it does not even exist.

Find your corner. Sit down, and learn to relax your physical body. You are to begin with this. You will not be concerned with how soon you can feel the magnetic current within your body, you will not be concerned with relaxing your mind, you will not be concerned with possible goals, but you will concentrate only upon relaxing your body.

If you have not done this before you will be puzzled as to just where you should begin. It is quite simple. You will give yourself a treatment for relaxation by speaking to yourself, either aloud or silently. It does not matter which. You will say to yourself, "I am beginning to relax completely. My toes are relaxed completely. My feet are relaxed completely. My legs are relaxed completely. My hips are relaxed completely. My chest is relaxed completely. My neck is relaxed completely. My head is relaxed completely." You will take a deep breath, let it out in a slow, easy manner, and you will find you are actually more relaxed than you were when you first sat down.

Now, sit there and think pleasant thoughts. You do not need to force anything into your mind. Picture a scene of beauty which brings enjoyment to you, recall some past event which was a happy one, or consider something to come in the future which gives you pleasure to contemplate. Whatever makes you happy is the subject you should carry in your mind. Take a deep breath every few moments and you will find that you are relaxing more and more as you sit. Plan upon doing this each day until your body relaxes the moment you have sat down, without any mental effort on your part.

Once your body is made still, you can begin the exercise of relaxing your mental processes. The mind does not *concentrate* upon this current to attain this accomplishment toward which you strive. The mind is trained into a subjective attitude, so the true intelligence can direct it as to what it is to think and how it is to operate.

You will begin relaxing your mind by doing exactly the same thing you did when you were sitting quietly and your body was learning to rest. Find, somewhere in the recesses of your mind, a picture which brings peace to you. Is it a lake, a waterfall? Is it a blue sky with white clouds floating in it? Is it a tall mountain? It does not matter. Find the picture which gives you a peaceful sensation.

Now, fasten your mind upon that picture, hold it without straining for as long as you can. When you feel that you are having to make an effort to keep it in your mind, let it go and you will know your exercise has ended for that time.

After you have learned to relax your body and your mind you will be ready for the greatest step of your life, because from that point on you will be going into the realms of the super physical, of the great beyond which has been such a mystery to most individuals on the human plane, and which will no longer be a mystery to you before you are through your seeking.

Assume you have now learned to relax. Your body is as quiet as it is in the night when you sleep. Your mind is a willing subject now, and is still.

Oh, but you say your mind does not wish to remain still; that in spite of your efforts it insists on speaking up, bringing to you memories of things which are of no importance, or remarking upon some subject in which you have no interest. Then, this is what you will do.

You will ignore your mind, just as an adult ignores a child who is insisting upon attention and is being naughty in order to get it. A child who has a temperamental tantrum cannot maintain that temper if he is ignored, and it is the same with your mind. Your physical mind is like a child. It needs to be directed, to be treated with kindness considered with love, but to be allowed no nonsense. So, if after a while it continues to refuse to lie quiescent while you seek the great intelligence beyond, simply ignore your mind as if it had not spoken to you, and go upon your way.

Now that you have relaxed, you will suddenly discover you are sitting in a stillness which you have not experienced before. It is so still you can almost hear it, and it separates you from your surroundings as if you were encased in cotton batting, or as if a glass wall were between you and the rest of your world.

When this silence becomes known to you, you will be permeated with such a peace, such an exalted peace,

21

you will be filled with the wonder of this one small example of what is in store for you. It will strengthen you for your material affairs, it will encourage you to continue your efforts toward understanding and self-improvement, and above all, it will make you newly aware of the great forces beyond the comparatively puny things you have known upon the earth, proving to you anew that God is indeed mighty beyond all.

You will sit in this peace and this silence for as long as your earthly affairs allow you to do so. Remember, it does not matter if you can only allow five minutes a day for this. If you can allow more time, it is well. But it does not matter. The important thing to remember is that you arrange to do this regularly, at the same time each day.

It is like learning to play the piano. Through exercises, through constant and regular practice, you become an accomplished musician; and likewise, through regular exercises and constant practice, you will become accomplished in the ability to turn the magnetic forces of the universe in any direction you wish to turn them.

When your material being is fully relaxed, you will be actively, actually in contact with the current. With practice, you can use this force in every part of your life.

THE LAW OF BALANCE

You have been living in a world which was created by Something or Somebody far beyond the ability of the human mind to imagine, and yet you have been attempting to live by standards which were set up by fellow human beings like yourself, whose minds lack the full wisdom of the Creator, lack the all-encompassing understanding with which he views his creation.

If you will learn to live by the basic laws of the universe, you will find your life is turned from the frustrated, unhappy and trapped condition you have suffered for years and is becoming free in a manner completely new to you.

Man was created to live by these basic laws, and automatically does so unconsciously while his conscious mind struggles to control his actions according to its conception of conformity. Thus he causes his own misery, since he was not intended to make his way through physical living by following a synthetic pattern of behavior.

Your modern civilization teaches you the habits of eating processed foods, of wearing uncomfortable clothing, of working at labors you do not enjoy, of pretending friendship with individuals you dislike; and following your active period in your younger days, you are taught that in your so-called declining years you must give up all things which would be of pleasure to you and must just sit, to wait for death.

Have you ever considered how lonely a physical being really is, if his material self is all he consists of, all there is to him? He is born alone. No matter how many assist at the birth, the baby himself arrives alone. He dies in the same manner.

Man stands in a crowded room and feels himself in such a solitude it frightens him. He stands in the midst of his own family and looks upon the faces of strangers. He seeks but he cannot find answers to great, unnamed longings within him, and no matter where he seeks the answers are elusive. They do not come to him. He asks the leader of his church, he asks his best friend, he asks the one closest to his heart. Sometimes he studies for many years and travels to the far places of the earth, and still he cannot find the answers which torture him so that very often he cannot sleep at night.

Is this the story of your life? Have you sought for answers which you have not found? Have you felt the loneliness and the longing which could not be described, and certainly have not yet been relieved? Then you may find that in following a path of blind faith for a short time you will discover a glorified way of living beyond anything you have known in the past.

"Blind faith" is merely an expression, because faith of course is never truly blind. In this instance the phrase is used to indicate the fact that if you are really seeking to understand yourself and to live with yourself in better harmony and more compassion, greater serenity, you must believe this *can* and *will* be accomplished even before you discover the methods by which you yourself can do it.

If you believe in a God of any kind, you have a faith with which to begin. It will not harm you to tell yourself you believe God will show you the way to exist as he intended you to exist, with happiness and fulfillment. You will tell yourself that because you cannot see these things which will come to you by way of understanding, you will believe without seeing. You will tell yourself that because you cannot touch the things which will come to you by way of understanding, you will believe they exist without touching.

Just as surely as you can see your own hand, just as surely as you can touch with your own fingers, you will understand how you may realize complete happiness, complete fulfillment. You can become the person you have always longed to be. You can find a position which is suited to your abilities and which will bring you contentment in your work. You can accomplish all of the goals which were created for the material plane and beyond that, you can go into the awareness of eternity which lies waiting for that moment when you pass through the great experience humanity has named death.

By employing the basic laws of creation, you will become as one with all things and therefore with the Creator. When there is only one thing, there can be nothing else, and because the Creator is all love, all power, all understanding, when you come to a sense of oneness you too will be all love, all power, all understanding. There is no question of this, because others have done it before you and will do it after you. Others are doing it now, and you have taken the first step by seeking in any way to know yourself.

The first thing you were told to remember was that you are no more and no less than anything else in creation. If you cannot persuade yourself of this in the beginning, at least you can continue to remind yourself that it is so until your human mind can accept a truth which it has been afraid to contemplate until now.

Everyone is different in his surface being, but beneath that surface there is an eternal self which is not only unchanging but is identical to, one with, all other eternal selves. This is God, and it cannot change, it cannot be different, it is a single unit working beautifully in harmony at all times. It only remains for the surface to become aware of the true activities which go on beneath that surface.

At first you may be confused. You will not know which impulse is a true one, you will not know what is truth and what is your imagination, you will not know what is intuition and what is education. But if you will have faith and will persevere, you will come to a time when you can choose between the real and the distorted. You will cease to look upon the past with longing, with sorrow or with regret. You will cease to look upon the future with fear, with impatience or with trepidation. You will live in the present, you will be happy, you will be contented, you will be grateful that you are living *now*.

Eternity is but a word, far beyond the comprehension of the unawakened mind. Its true meaning is simple. It means n-o-w. There was no yesterday, there will be no tomorrow, there is only now. If you will begin to pattern your life upon this fact, you will at once find a happier and an easier sensation entering your physical being.

When you awaken in the morning, you are born. *Now* it is a new day. You have opportunities to accomplish, to correct distortions, to do anything you wish to do because you are living now and there is no other time.

At night, when the day is ended and you are going to sleep, let your last thought be, *now* I rest. I am grateful for the opportunities of the day, I am grateful that now the day is over and I can rest.

The following morning you will be born again, and so it is with each day and night of your physical existence, because when you awaken in the morning it is the same as the awakening of a child when it first comes into the world. When you go to sleep at night, it is the same as the death of a physical shell when an individual is finished with it.

You have been dormant in many ways or you would not have a need to seek. You have followed suggestions of others, and perhaps their orders too, in many ways. You may have listened to the words of those who speak soothingly and convincingly. Perhaps you have read the words of those who write glibly and easily, or have watched those who act with great ability, so great you believed their acting to be real.

Now it is time you became an individual. Follow the promptings of your own heart. Listen to it. It will speak to you; not the organ you are in the habit of considering as your heart, which drives the blood through your body, but the inner heart of you, the core of you, which you may call the voice of God. Listen to it. It speaks swiftly and only once. Learn to consult this inner voice. You have it, just as all others have it. Because you have not been aware of it does not mean that it has no existence.

You have undoubtedly had hunches or a flash of intuition from time to time which proved to be completely true, completely correct. This is the inner self speaking, and call it what you will, it is still the same force in operation.

You may use this force in business, to make decisions,

to seek out the answers to all phases of human living. Sometimes it is necessary to go beyond the plane of mortality in order to find the key to happy living within the mortal dimension. This is the reason you are asked to believe from the very beginning that you can and will accomplish whatever you seek to accomplish as long as you trust, as long as you have honest motives, as long as you do not falter at the scoffings of others or accept the advice of others.

If you will keep your search a secret, you will find that the results are far greater than if you attempt to share them with those who do not have an understanding of what you seek. Remember this: You are alone in the world as a human being because you are completely individual, but you are never *really* alone because God is with you, and if you will cling to this thought, you will find you have learned to live with harmony.

The basic laws apply to everything in creation. Since there are no exceptions, the sooner you can learn that the laws are absolute truth and can follow them in your daily existence, the sooner you will reach serenity and accomplishment upon your surface living.

The workings of the laws are mysteries beyond your comprehension. The how of them, even the when, you will not discover while you inhabit a physical body, but you can discover their existence by observing them in action all about you any time, and you can then accept the truth that they do work for everything. When you can free your consciousness of your material being, you will easily find the answers to the riddle of the basic laws.

You have been wondering, perhaps, what these basic

laws are. There is much reference to them among the individuals who are seeking, and some who feel they have already found what they seek, but so few seem to know just what they are. This is not because they are mysteries beyond knowing, but because most individuals cannot accept *what* the laws are without an accompanying explanation as to *how* they operate.

If you can accept the law of balance, that each thing is balanced by another thing, you are far ahead in your journey toward understanding. If you think you must learn how these things balance, when they are balanced, if you question beyond your human ability to absorb, you are holding yourself from another forward step. You must remember that trust does not need to be accompanied by a clear vision. Trusting that accomplishment will be made is enough to send you on your way. Because the material mind inclines to lose itself in the mazes of thought, it is best if you do not question the how's and the why's and only accept the fact of "is," the truth of *is*.

How does the law of balance apply to you? Exactly as it applies to everything else in creation. If you help another by giving something, whether it is of monetary value or of the values beyond price, your giving will be balanced at another time by a receiving. If you give grudgingly and only because you feel you can not gracefully refuse to give, then at some future time when you have need of help the same begrudging attitude will be shown to you so you may learn through this balancing that giving is a giving of self, that giving is truly a sharing, and that when something changes hands with a distorted attitude involved, it is not giving at all.

When you give supply to one who is in need and you

29

give it only to rid yourself of the individual's presence, you are not giving anything. You are taking from that individual his dignity, his need as a fellow human being, and you are rejecting him as a part of your self, which he is and which you cannot escape. Every worthwhile deed you perform is balanced by your receiving worthwhile things in return. Every shameful deed you perform is balanced by your receiving shameful deeds in return. ("Shameful" is the expression familiar to the physical plane. "Distorted" is the correct expression, for a deed less than perfect is a distortion of perfection, nothing else.) Because all things are one, whatever you do you are doing to yourself.

And so it goes without end, as *you* are without end, everything balancing itself in the right time according to the plan of the Supreme Intelligence. Be comforted by this fact. Do not be frightened by it, do not be resentful of it, and do not be fatalistic toward it to the extent you will say, "What is the use in my trying? Whatever 1 do, I cannot gain unless I help someone else to gain." Your efforts are rewarded, regardless of what they might be. Whatever it is you do, the great channel of power brings back to you that which you have poured into it.

Comfort yourself with this, because it means that while you alone are responsible for every experience you encounter, for every happiness, every misery; for every success, every setback; for every understanding, every ignorance; for every friend, every enemy; likewise you are not responsible for anyone else.

If you are a parent, you may feel responsible for your child's destiny. This is not true. Your sole responsibility to a child is to protect and to cherish until that child is ready to take his place in the world as a self-reliant adult. It is not your place to shield him from experiences which must come to every individual. It is not your place to assume guilt for experiences which come to a child due to his own actions. You must help in any way you can if you would fulfill to the utmost your great opportunity as a parent. But this child has had experiences which must be balanced in his own path, and you must understand this that you can help him to understanding.

If you have parents who are dependent upon you for their daily food and their shelter, it does not mean you are responsible for their actions nor are you responsible for their reactions to what you are doing.

If you are a friend, you are not responsible for the actions of your friends, but you are only responsible for your own attitude of friendship, of assistance if it is requested of you, if it is needed.

If you are an employer, you are responsible solely for the manner in which you operate, the consideration you give your employees. If you are an employee, you are responsible only for what you give to your position. You are not responsible for the laxity of fellow workers or for the fact that some of them perhaps can do work more quickly or more efficiently than you have been doing it.

Your basic, primary, and in the ultimate conclusion *sole* responsibility is to your self, for this is God, everything; not in a selfish manner, that you should shut out the rest of your world and consider only your surface self in all things, but that you must be true to that within you which is attempting to guide you at all times.

In whatever relationship you experience upon the planet Earth, you are responsible only for what you give to that

31

relationship, for what you take from it. Everyone else must handle his own giving and taking. This is the law of balance. What goes up must come down. What goes out must come in. What turns left must turn right. What goes forth must come back. All things are balanced regardless of their manifestation. Whether they are human beings, animals, trees or grains of sand, they are existing under the law of balance and they too must balance each awareness, each thing they do or think or accomplish or do not accomplish.

Remember this if you would feel guilty when you are innocently involved in some action due to another individual's activities and not yours. Regardless of surface appearances in the beginning, you will not have upon your record any mark if you have done nothing distorted. You may be falsely accused in the material world, but if you steadfastly cling to the knowledge of the truth that the innocent shall *not* suffer with the guilty, you will not suffer. If you have a past deed which requires balancing you will balance it no matter how hard you try to escape it, no matter how much you rebel against it.

You cannot blame anyone for anything which comes to you unless you wish to blame yourself. If you do this you will halt your progress toward self-understanding and self-acceptance because when you blame you accuse, when you accuse you have already condemned, when you condemn you do not love, and you must love your self as the great Creator if you will reach fulfillment in every way, in any way.

Balance yourself by a calm contemplation of your daily actions, balance your life by a happy acceptance of all experiences which come to you, for each one is contributing to your understanding, your wisdom, your ultimate achievement of awareness of oneness with God.

You cannot reach that oneness without balance, and once you have achieved balance you cannot maintain it unless you remember you and you alone can keep your days in serenity and your nights in peace.

The law of balance has been called by many names. It has been described in many ways by the master ones who have come to the planet Earth over a period of many thousands of years. To the Christian religion it is known as the Golden Rule. This is the major law of creation, and if you can accept this one law, learn to apply it to your life, you will have no need for seeking out the other basic laws.

The great teachers expressed this truth in many ways to fit their particular periods of time, their particular languages and their particular students. But it has always remained the same truth—that you receive in like measure to that you would give; that you should do toward others that which you would prefer having done toward you. This law applies to every part of your world, to every part of your being. It *is* the law of balance.

It is a sad fact that most individuals of the human world are familiar with this Golden Rule, but do not apply it in their own lives, not realizing it is a basic part of their existence. They consider it a beautiful thought, a wonderful idea, but impractical and not for them because they have been living under the misunderstanding that if they treat others with kindness, consideration, love, they are being fools, for others will mistreat them in return; that the only way to get safely through life is with a belligerent attitude, an enmity in human relations as a protection against possible mistreatment by others.

If you are kind to your fellow beings but you kick an animal, you have expressed yourself in a distorted fashion and the law of balance will bring that kick back to you at some time. It may not be a physical blow, but it will cause the same reaction in you that you caused in the animal. If you mistreat a flower, although you give consideration to your fellow human beings you are expressing in a distorted fashion and you in turn will be mistreated, met with cruelty, and perhaps will wonder why when you have been so kind, you must receive such treatment.

If you would be different to the masses of suffering humanity, to the misery which enfolds so much of the world today, live with the law of balance until it becomes your constant expression. Teach yourself, your mind, to accept the fact that there are no exceptions to the laws of creation, there are no mistakes committed by these laws, there are no escapes from the consequences of your own deeds. Your motives are the reasons behind your actions and your motives will be balanced by return actions in time. You reward yourself, you punish yourself, you move yourself forward in the search toward enlightenment or you hold yourself back to a snail's pace.

You—you do all of these, no one and no thing else. God does not watch your every move, waiting to pounce upon you with punishment if you digress from the path of righteousness. God does not become angry with you if you make a mistake (distort a truth). The Creator established the laws when he caused countless parts of himself to express in the material planes, and these laws work automatically, without need for anything other than yourself to cause them to move.

You trigger the action, which then becomes inevitable in its function. Like putting a coin into a perfectly-operating machine, you push a certain button and you get for that coin the product of the button you have pushed. The machine itself does not choose. It does not give you extra or withold from you any part of what you have purchased. This is the way the laws work. You push the button, you pay the coin, and you receive in like measure the amount you have paid, you receive the product whose button you have pushed.

You need not blame yourself for past actions or even for present ones because they were or are distortions of perfection. You have only to keep within you always the reminder of the law of balance. You cannot falter or fail in any way because you are the beautiful, living proof there is a God, there is perfection, and you are as ready to express that perfection as any part of creation.

YOUR SURFACE BEING

You cannot aim at a high goal and expect to reach it in one leap, unless you have prepared yourself, have trained your muscles that they can take you to this high goal with the first attempt.

In the physical past, you may not even have climbed a low fence in an effort toward self-understanding, toward expressing *you*, so do not expect to suddenly leap the highest mountain because you have reached the point of wanting to understand yourself and all things of God.

Take each step as it comes to you individually, in your own order. Once you have begun the process of becoming still, it may be months before the grandeur of realization comes to you, or you may reach awareness of mighty truths beyond your world immediately.

Whatever your path to understanding may be, always remember you must be patient. The Supreme Intelligence knows the best time for your unfoldment and the correct degree of that unfolding. You will not develop your understanding more swiftly than your mind can accept it, handle it. If you did, your human self would reject truth, delaying its coming and making it doubly difficult for you to accept at a later date. Truth will come to you wherever you are, in the right time, if you will be still and allow it to make itself known.

In your particular world, the only things that seem to have reality are those matters to which you give your attention. Although there are other activities, other events, they do not exist for you unless you have directed your attention to them.

The condition of your physical being depends on this attention, depends on whether you have a clear perspective of your bodily functions, your reasons for having a material vehicle, or a distorted attitude toward surface existence in general.

Your physical body is your responsibility. While you are expressing in a material dimension, you are expected to care for your particular surface self just as you would attend to any machine which performed functions, tasks, for you.

While the physical body is an expression of God, it is not much more than a robot by itself. Just as your voice is an expression of your vocal chords but by itself has no ability to direct its actions, your body, robot to the Master Mind within, responds to the manipulations of this intelligence according to its condition, its maintenance. If you keep your surface being clean, comfortable and healthy, it will respond to your every prompting immediately and precisely. If it has been neglected or abused it will respond accordingly.

A robot, gone out of control, would move aimlessly, inevitably destroying or at least damaging anything in its path. You would not condemn the robot for this, because you would understand it can do nothing of itself but must be guided, directed, kept in perfect running order, if it is to operate as it was built to operate.

The unawakened human person is like the robot out of control. He damages or destroys whatever he contacts, but he cannot be condemned because *he does not know what he is doing.* When he is aware consciously of his place in the scheme of creation, his concern is automatic, instituted by his sense of oneness. He is careful to direct his actions, avoiding hurt to others.

Therefore, do not criticize yourself if you have been aimlessly traveling through physical life, not knowing where you are going or how to get there. Without awareness, your mind could not operate your own physical body, your robot, without some distortion.

As you seek to know your self, as you journey toward awareness, *you* can take control of your surface being and guide it so it will do what it is intended to do. You can keep it in good working order by regular cleansing, regular feeding, regular attention to it according to the pattern of your destiny.

As you take step after step into the light of the knowing, keep with you the memory of your own falterings in darkness that you do not misunderstand the falterings of others. Remember that *no* seemingly terrible deed or apparently stupid action is taken by a knowing one. You do not revile an infant if its aimless hand knocks over a glass and breaks it; you understand the infant has not yet learned control. So it is with the "infants" of the mortal world. You will remember, as you go your way, that they have simply not yet learned how to be undistorted expressions of God. It will help you toward your own awareness, for in giving your understanding to unawakened consciousnesses of others, understanding from the Center of all creation comes to your mind more easily.

Your surface body is, as you know, an intricate machine, designed with delicacy, beauty and utilitarianism. Not one part is useless, not one part is out of place, not one part is less important than any other part. Individuals who study the body from a totally intellectual point of view might disagree, but you realize this is true, or will realize it as you understand everything does have equal importance to everything else in creation.

You cannot care for your face and ignore care of your feet if you are to be the full expression of your inner self. You cannot eat your fill, then neglect to slake your thirst if you are to maintain your material balance. You are expected to give your material being the respect and the concern you would give to anyone or anything in your care.

The human being is only reflecting what it is capable of allowing to come through to that surface self. When it is trained to reflect beauty from within, that is what it will show. When it is in its very best condition, it will be ready to reflect to its fullest degree, to the fullest degree the consciousness can accept, the inner self, the eternal, perfect one.

You undoubtedly have at least one physical characteristic of which you have been or are ashamed, which you may even have regarded with loathing. Since you are at present expressing through a human plane, your physical mind may not have been trained to transmit clearly, and so your physical self probably thinks it is much less than perfect.

If this is so, doubtlessly at times you have wished you were someone else, at least in appearance. You probably think others regard you with disrespect, with scorn or with ridicule, because of your surface characteristics. This may have been the situation until now, but the reason has not been due to any physical "defects". Others accept you as you accept yourself, as your human mind regards itself and its outside appearance. As long as you *think* defects and inferiority, you will *express* this lack of understanding in your surface person. Others, because as earth-expressions they also misunderstand, accept you as being that which is your presentation of yourself.

This is especially for you, dearest friend. It is offered with deep love, with understanding of your human emotions about your seeming defects, with understanding of your human emotions about your seeming lack of ability, your "uninteresting" personality, your "idiosyncrasies". Leave your despair and step into the joyous knowledge that you are all you dream of being, for dreams are the stirrings of truth from within, setting into motion the action of reflecting reality on the outer plane.

In the surface dimension, the physical characteristics of every part of your world vary widely. They differ in so many ways that even upon one small planet in creation the unaware cannot accept all the differences, cannot understand there is no ugliness, nothing ludicrous. How bewildered, even frightened would these be if they could behold the continuing wonders and varieties of God's kingdom!

Since the Creator is all that exists, the variations in the material worlds must be all right, *every one of them*. God cannot be wrong or mistaken in one infinitesimal part of his creation, or he is totally all wrong, mistaken. He *is* the one total in existence, the Allness of all.

There is charm, fascination, allure, beauty in every physical expression of God. The untrained mind, the unawakened awareness, does not recognize these qualities, just as an uneducated individual would not realize the material worth of a diamond found encrusted with dirt. Such lack of recognition does not alter the truth; it simply deflects the visions of those who will not see it.

40

You are beautiful. When your present vehicle is prepared and trained to express that beauty, your surface self will also be beautiful. When you express the truth within you, you will be a beautiful individual. Do not be afraid of or ashamed of beauty. A beautiful man is completely masculine in his expression of that God-self which makes him so wonderful to behold. A beautiful woman is completely feminine in her expression of that God-being which makes her so irresistible. Age has nothing to do with this, size has nothing to do with it, no material characteristic has anything to do with it. These are *reflections* only, not cause but effect.

Some of the most magnetic, most beautiful individuals have "irregular" features, "misshapen" bodies, physical attributes which would be termed "ugly" by material standards. But their inner lights, shining radiantly upon the material world, transform everything about them so the irregular features are handsome, the misshapen bodies are symmetrical, the ugly attributes are most attractive.

Lack of understanding is the one, the *only* cause for all of the physical world's upset, unhappy conditions. Those who understand, who *feel* the truth, cannot be miserable, cannot upset or be upset under any circumstances. Why? Because they are so full of the love that is awareness they have no room in them for anything else, not even enough room to squeeze in one small distortion.

Once you understand there is intelligent cause for variation in the features of all faces—God's intelligent cause—, you will accept your own features and forget you ever considered them unpleasing. This will be true of all your surface self, because you will understand there

41

is also intelligent reason for variations in size, in color, in personality. There is *no* intelligent reason for criticism or ridicule of someone who does not fit the exact mold of the popular pattern. Ignorance breeds distortion of love, expressed by unthinking words and deeds. These reactions deny the very existence of a Creator, for they declare the characteristics of some parts of the mortal dimension are not as they should be, and so pronounce God is not perfect, which he must be if he exists at all.

Unfortunately, it is widely accepted in the *un*-understanding parts of the earth plane that certain features are pleasing and others are repulsive, that certain sizes are attractive and others are unattractive. The standard is set up according to the general characteristics of the majority. It is seldom noted that handsome faces on the northern side of the world are almost directly opposite in appearance to handsome faces on the southern side of the world; that while small people may be an ideal size in the east big people are probably ideal in the west.

There is variation to fit every human inclination, to express the numberless characteristics of God. Your human self never need be ashamed of any part of your physical being. You are *exactly right* at this moment. What you will become tomorrow or next year will be exactly right also. You need never be ashamed if someone else considers you unattractive, because only ignorance would mark you as anything except just right. When you openly express the truth within you, you will become truly beautiful, not merely attractive, and no longer *un*-attractive, even to those who have not reached understanding.

Keep in mind that the most symmetrical features in

your world do not produce beauty. They are a pleasure to behold, but they are not beauty. This *must* come from within. It is the fountain of eternity, the flow of God, the light of love. It cannot be copied, it cannot be assumed. It *is,* and that is a fact indestructible and unremovable.

Whether or not you have so-called "regular" features in your present pattern, you will be beautiful when you begin allowing your love-self to express through your surface. Beauty, like everything else without exception, is the expression of love, which is thoroughly, completely overpowering.

You may think at present that some feature of your face is so prominent or irregular no one can see past it to find *you,* but in truth, when you become what you are meant to be, no one will notice any lack of proportion, for that lack will no longer exist. That feature fits you as an individual. It is right for you, and you would not be the same person with another. When you are expressing your true beauty, your features will be fully beautiful, every one, because they are a part of your expression.

Understand this, that you may realize how it is no physical characteristic can mar the mirroring of your inner perfection. Every inch of your body, every pore of your skin, is a *reflection,* a physical expression of the extent to which *you* are free to shine forth with your glorious splendor. The brighter the light, the more attractive the vehicle transmitting its glow will be, the stronger the magnetism of the human person.

You are so much more than a physical body, you are much more than the surface appearance of the husk which will survive in its present form only to the end of your material journey. When you are being what you truly are, the shell, your physical self, *must* follow the lead of *you*. It has no other choice, no other reason for having been created. This is how your surface can be transformed from seeming plainness to beauty, from seeming ugliness to magnetism. It is not only possible but inevitable, following the law of creation.

When your mind knows the truth that *you* are complete perfection and that your human personality can express that perfection, you will open to the directions from the Eternal Intelligence which will adjust your surface to undistorted reflection of God-self.

You do not immediately change your usual daily schedule when revelation comes to you. You are not supposed to drop all your labors, your activities, once you consciously realize and allow your inner being to guide your life. You follow the pattern, when awakening comes, which is familiar to you. You follow it with a changed attitude, not a changed action, knowing all right experiences will be yours without effort.

You do not search the world to find the truth, once you realize all of creation is contained in your own being. You do not literally sit without moving, waiting for all things to come to you. You continue to work, to play, to do whatever you ordinarily do. The change, during the early part of your journey to open expression of self, will be in your mental attitude, with your happy anticipation, your aware acceptance.

You will have no envy for the talents or abilities of anyone else, no desire for the material possessions of others. You will have so much you will have no time for consideration of what others have, no time for observing the so-called flaws or seemingly special attributes of others. It is not in the pattern of destiny that all should express by the same means, so you will not have a need for or an urge to try everything in the material world. You, as an individual expression, will be inclined in certain directions, and when awareness has opened your mind, if you find apparently new talents available, it will only be because you were not awake to your abilities before. These will be the talents *you* wish to express in your present lifetime.

There are no limits for you in appearance, ability, anything else on earth. Regardless of your past expression, you are truly an individual with endless capability. Your human mind is limited only to the extent it has convinced itself it has boundaries. Since your mind is the transmitter for your supreme intelligence, which is eternal, everything, it follows that your mind must also have endless capacity, never-ending ability, that your human self is capable of anything, of everything, once you realize how mighty the inner *you*, the God-soul, is.

If you have had moments of despair, if you have thought and even now are thinking, "These things are wonderful, but *I* cannot do them because I do not have intelligence or ability," bring yourself comfort and encouragement. Never again say to yourself that you are limited in any way, because if you do, you are speaking a lie, a distortion, to the individual who is the most important person in your existence at this moment. It is not a truth, so do not express such a statement.

Your mind may have seemed limited, confined, in the past, but it was not because you lack supreme intelligence.

45

Your appearance may have seemed less than beautiful, magnetic, in the past, but it was not because you lack any of the qualities of beauty. All that prevented your being as capable, as attractive as anyone else was your misunderstanding, your unknowingness of truth. Your human self, the robot, the *expression* of God, not the *source* of his power, was not being directed, controlled, by *you*, the eternal God.

There can be nothing without reason, nothing without God, so you have *every* reason within you for being anything wonderful, for being all there is. When you accept the prompting of your true intelligence toward your mind, when you transmit the intuitional impulses from your true being, nothing can stop your becoming whatever you are impelled to become in the mortal dimension. Then, you do not choose your path with selfishness, you do not determine your destiny with indifference to others, you do not decide anything haphazardly. You operate from the core, the focal point of your being, all love, all intelligence. Your human self *can not* distort this control once it is fully in charge.

You will find you are expressing with more individuality than ever when you find your self. You *should* be individual, different, and if you are already different, you are a step further on the path to expression of self than those who try to be carbon copies of everyone else.

Individuality is God's way of expressing his own self, and it has been thus forever, before time came into being on the material plane. Individuality is God's way of expressing the endlessness of his might, the scope of his power.

Once you accept realization, understand individuality

and its cause, it will be simple for you to have the courage to be that which you find within you. Courage is only another word for knowing. In knowing truth you cannot be afraid, having nothing to fear, therefore you are courageous.

You are blessed when you are set apart, for every great one has and does walk alone consciously. Knowing each thing of creation must make its own way back to the Creator is a warmth to hold close in the loneliness of the solitary journey to God. Beyond the loneliness of the human mind, you will some day find the ecstasy in aloneness, for it will come to you that this is the ultimate oneness with That which permeates all things.

You can seem to be rejected by the ignorant for some surface difference, but you will not *accept* rejection if you realize ignorance expresses make-believe emotions, and fear is foremost among these. The ignorant are fearful of all they do not understand, and since they understand very little, they are often and much afraid. You who know will feel compassion for the unknowing in their prejudices, understanding their turning away from you is caused by their fear, fear of your strength, of your magnetism. They can feel this but their minds cannot produce an acceptable explanation for it so they draw back, covering their human trepidations, false in that they are distorted, with another distortion called ostracism.

You are so beloved of God it would be impossible for you to have any characteristics which would make you repulsive. It would be impossible for you to have any characteristics which would make you less lovable than others, less wanted in Creation's great circle. You are equally regarded in your surface appearance, in your

47

abilities, with everything else which expresses in any world, yours or those beyond yours, throughout the entire creation. The knowing ones so regard you, the knowing ones call you beloved.

Nothing is impossible to God. For this reason, as his expression, you can gain respect, admiration, understanding from your fellow beings even though you may have gained none of these before today. When you are determined to express your inner beauty, when *you* command your human mind to obey you, that inner self will show through your surface person and nothing can prevent your being beautiful. Everything balances itself, everything corrects itself when beauty is freed, for it transforms everything it touches into a mirror of itself.

Beauty, the love glowing from within and casting a spell upon any beholder, will transform the most deviating physical expression. Beauty, the love that is God expanding from the center of your being, will give real, actual physical charm to any individual. The most rugged male, the daintiest female, will become beautiful in his or her individual way when inner self becomes outer expression undistorted by surface unawareness.

Appearance is not the only characteristic of the inner you, striving to make itself known to the outer world. It seems most important because human beings have made it so, have enlarged it beyond all reason and made it a tragic despot over many. Entire lives have been distorted because lack of understanding caused self-repugnance, because the unawakened accept the equally unawakened opinions of others.

When you have fitted your appearance into its proper place, you will have joined it to all other physical characteristics of your life-phase. No less, no more than any part of your dimensional world, appearance, you will find, adjusts itself without conscious attention from you as you grow in the direction of your own sublimity.

Your condition also is affected by your understanding of truth. If you maintain fears, resentments, worries, you plant seeds of distortion in your physical mind. These must be dissolved or expressed, and your body being the vehicle for your expression, will be beset with ills and ailments unless you remove the festers at once.

If the mind has been allowed to disregard its directions, if it has not been taught discipline but is running wildly about of its own free will, you will have absorbed or collected items of emotion, of experience, of reaction which upset you mentally. It might be anger at a fellow worker, it might be envy of a neighbor's new property, it might be resentment that you are not appreciated as much as you think you should be. If this is allowed to remain in the mind it soon must find an outlet, and the outlet for the brain is the body.

An illness or an ailment comes upon the body as a result of a festered spot within the mind. If you would cure yourself you must cure the cause and not the effect. You can go to a doctor and receive a treatment. If you have complete faith that the doctor will cure you you will be cured, but it is your faith in that doctor and his methods and not what he does. If you would turn within and seek the spot in your mind to rid yourself of this condition, your physical ailment would disappear and you would be completely well again.

There is no illness in the mortal world which is other than the result of a synthetic emotion, a distortion of

49

reality, mind-confused. Any suffering can be alleviated the instant the individual who suffers is awakened to understanding God does not experience suffering, illness, or anything except love. It is only the surface expressions which go through agonies, inconveniences, experiencing unreal sensations as strongly as if they existed. The self does not experience anything except love. It cannot, since that love, God, is all of its substance.

Those who have sustained fear or have lived with daily tensions chaining them often express these distortions through the condition known as cancer. If they would awaken to realizing relaxation is the secret of balanced physical maintenance, and if they would overcome, disintegrate fear, they would be healed.

Those who have clung to resentment, envy, sometimes express through conditions such as arthritis, bursitis or neuralgia. These are also caused often by suppression of human self over a long period of time. When these individuals can understand God does not resent, when they love instead of envy, when they stop living like prisoners on the surface plane, they will be healed.

These are examples of the diseases prevalent today, a very few of the many. Regardless of its nature, nothing in the world of mortals is incurable because it is only a product of that world and can be found nowhere else. When eternal love, truth, the great current of God, is tuned in, any mortal distortion is disintegrated. Unless an individual insists on clinging to his unreal emotions, he *cannot* be ill.

Do these seem heartless statements to you? They are not meant to be so. The eye of truth, turned in any direction, does not inspire criticism, advice or indifference;

only love. Love, contrary to many opinions, sees with a clear, straight vision. It is *not* blind. The human mind has mistaken it as such because it is all-understanding and so does not make any effort to change, to remonstrate, to belittle.

Health is more than a state of mind. It is an expression of being, a manifestation of the mind's proper functioning as a transmitter for real intelligence. Respond to your supreme self and your human mind will operate smoothly. Operate your mind smoothly and your body will be maintained properly. The directions to your body from your brain are *instituted* by your true intelligence. If transmitted correctly, these directions keep your body working perfectly, in perfect health.

When past distortions have produced present situations wherein sustained illness or physical weakness is expressed, the situations can be balanced the instant they are understood. Understanding erases karmic debt, which is a series of lessons necessary for an upward step toward enlightenment. Once a truth is realized, further "study" becomes superfluous, and the Great Intelligence does nothing which is unnecessary.

You have probably been taught that physical ailments are things which cannot be helped, that some people are simply less robust than others and so have less resistance to disease. Is it not odd to you that as civilization progresses scientifically, that as the pace of your living is stepped up, new diseases are discovered, new medicines must be developed to treat them, new methods must be found with which to overcome these diseases?

Consider it and you will see that the new diseases are simply products of the human mind, which has been stirred

51

to a fresh apprehension by the news about destructive bombs, stirred to another fear by the threats of belligerent countries, stirred to new terror by the fact that your skies are filled with ships which come from an unknown source and are piloted by unknown individuals.

In each age of man new diseases have developed, because in each age there are new developments in civilization itself. In the reactions to these developments man creates a condition within his body of distortion which must in turn express itself, for each thing must act in some way and it must express through the vehicle to which it is connected.

You can maintain a balanced state of physical wellbeing and a mental serenity by giving your attention to truth. If distortion begins to slip into your mind with fear—worry, resentment, greed—, fill yourself so full of God the distortion cannot find room for entrance.

If you have some material condition which causes you discomfort, pain, inconvenience, realize you have this condition because of some unknowing expression by your physical mind. Lack of understanding is the only cause for anything less than perfection in your body, in your world. Lack of understanding is love unawakened.

This is fact, not fancy, and if you will accept it, act accordingly whenever you have an ailment of any kind, the consequences of your acceptance will prove the truth. You can be cured, you can remain perfectly healthy, and you can do it yourself. You have the strength, the ability to perform so-called miracles such as any master ones have shown to your world.

It does not matter whether you have a cold, whether you are paralyzed, whether you have been told your days are few. Nothing matters except the truth, that when your time to leave the physical vehicle has come, you can leave it in perfect health, you need not deteriorate in any way before you go. The physical body can be perfect in its mechanism, in its operation, if you will get into the habit of maintaining it perfectly. First you must readjust whatever is out of balance due to former misunderstanding upon your part, and then you must maintain that balance through a constant awareness of your reactions to the outer things which go on about you.

If another becomes angry with you, refuse to anger in return, because if you do you have planted a physical disability within your mind and eventually it will be expressed in some form by distorted conditions in your body. Nothing and no one can affect your physical condition except you, and regardless of what happens to others about you, you can be untouched by anything if you will take the steps to protection for yourself.

Repeat many times, "Because *I* am perfect, my body and mind are perfect. Because *I* have no emotion but only the feeling of love, my surface being has only love emotions. Because *I* know that God is all, my physical mind and body respond to that truth by overlooking any ignorance upon the part of others who do not have this understanding, and by giving them, in return for whatever they give me, my understanding."

You are moving toward your goal of eternal oneness constantly, so do not think you are stupid or remiss because of any unawakened awareness. When you know all, understand all, you will be something other than a Godself expressing through a physical body.

Until you come to the point beyond the necessity for

incarnating in a dimension such as your present one, accept your unknowing acts as the lessons not yet learned in your school of creation. When you begin recognizing that such acts are unknowing, or distorted, you are a long way toward the point where you will know complete truth.

Your illnesses, your afflictions, can exist only as long as you want them to do so. When you refuse them, truly reject them with *feeling,* not just with wishful thinking, they will be gone.

One ailment is no more or less than another ailment. The dreaded diseases of your world are exactly the same as the common inconveniences, both reflecting untrue misunderstandings. A plague results from concerted ignorance expressed by large numbers of individuals. One infected organ results from ignorance expressed by one individual. So it goes with any condition in the physical plane. Control your emotions, direct your mind, and you will express health, vitality, attractiveness. Give way to the custom of distortion, to which so many have been educated, let your mind follow the usual physical aimlessness and you will express illness, weakness, unattractiveness.

Your physical condition is as simple as that. It ties to all other phases of expression, fastened in oneness with everything of the material dimension. Full expression of the withinness produces perfection in any part of living, unawareness of the inner existence produces distortion in every part of living.

You will notice beauty added to all parts of your surface atmosphere when you open to God. His greatness spreads equally, so your appearance, your health, your comfort will respond in equal parts. There is no real necessity for concentrating your efforts to understand on one area of your life. When you discover another facet of truth, realize it and so accept it, that truth automatically follows the laws of God and expresses itself in the plane created solely for that purpose.

However, because individual needs differ, because individual understanding differs, many openings are made. If a person cannot grasp the meaning of the statement that God, being all, perfects all physical things at once as he is recognized, that person can still find his own self through concentrating his understanding on any one part of God's power.

You can follow any path your intuition takes you along, and it will be right, perfect for you. You will not be less than some because you concentrate on one specific point of truth, nor will you be more than others because you can grasp the overall truth and open to it.

Just remember that any part of your surface expression is nothing, can be nothing, other than a reflection of what you want it to be. If you have seemed to be indifferent in the past to some phase of your daily life, there has been reason. Nothing is senseless, haphazard in truth, so your seeming indifference must have been due to the need for you to bring your attention more strongly to other phases. As you awaken spiritually, you see all about you, all at once. You appreciate, savor, revel in, are grateful for everything characterizing the material world and your place in it. You feel wonderful physically, you think clearly, and you are a happy individual.

You can make your human self whatever is correct for it to be, by letting that self go to show itself to the mortal world. *You* can keep your physical vehicle in marvelous condition by filling it with awareness to such an extent it throbs and glows with it. *You* can, do and will perform your destined assignments in this dimension without interference, by permeating with your awareness the mind of your material embodiment.

Your surface self is all that *you* are, potentially if you have not been aware of this truth, fully if you have realized it.

Your years do not matter, your circumstances do not matter, nothing matters except that God exists in you as fully as he exists in all parts of his kingdom.

Know this for yourself, and you will be physically beautiful, radiantly healthy, completely all you are intended to be.

COLOR AND MUSIC

Color is a wonderful part of your life. It is a reflection of your moods and characteristics, of your condition. It is the most important factor when you choose clothing, decorative schemes for your living quarters, background for your work.

Every part of your physical body is some color, varying in shade from every other part, so no two organs, no two veins, no two atoms are exactly the same. The colors of your body reflect your spiritual being, to the extent the inner beauty has been freed to express by your mind.

Your personal response to color is geared to your awareness. If you are bright and gay, your favorite colors are bright and gay. If you are quiet and calm, your favorite colors are quiet and calm too. You can show any preference you wish on the surface, but your actual preferences will be toward the colors which harmonize with you.

You may have observed how some colors tend to depress you, while others give you a surge of energy or a happy feeling. Memories of past lives, unrecognized though they are, influence your reactions in the present lifetime. Unhappy experiences will cause strong aversions to certain places, certain individuals, certain colors. Happy experiences will draw you toward the individuals involved or to those who have some characteristic which reminds you of past events. You will feel completely at home in places you have not seen before in this lifetime, and your favorite colors will include those which were outstanding in your past happiness.

If your mind is not yet aware of the beauty of creation itself, it will be unaware of the beauties on the material plane. If your mind is not yet conscious of the oneness of the eternal, it will not be conscious of the individuality of the temporal.

Color is a reflection of *you* also, based on the distortion or clarity of your material understanding. When you free your true being, your true colors will be drawn to you automatically, following the natural law of like attracting like.

All colors are love colors, for they are God expressing another delight for the eyes to behold, another strength for the body to build with, another awareness to which the intuition will respond. It is not necessary to see a color physically to be made aware of its particular appeal and purpose. With your eyes closed you can touch different colors and find they feel different to your fingers. Holding very still, you can sense various colors moving about you, be aware of their different vibrations.

Your best colors will keep you serene, balanced, if you respond to their message, their reasons for expression through you. You can improve your health, your comfort, contribute to your success, your happiness, by living with color to an harmonious degree.

Everything created as individual expression in the material dimension must learn to work with everything else, become aware of and make use of all that is at hand. You, a human being, must learn to operate in harmony with everything in your atmosphere. If you do not, you slow your own steps and hamper the actions of whatever you ignore. Flowers cannot express their beauty freely if you will not give them your attention. Stars cannot shine as brightly if you will not raise your head. Music cannot sound as sweetly if you will not listen. Color cannot give its power if you will not open to it. Become aware of color, of what it will do for and with you, and you have in your possession another of the world's great treasures. Specifically, you have another tool with which to work, another strength with which to accomplish.

For regular vitalizing influence, you can give your physical body treatments in color. You will contribute to an overall condition of calmness, of conscious awareness, by surrounding yourself with blue. Use lights, sit in a blue room, or go outdoors, where your ceiling is more beautiful than anything man has produced.

If you need renewed energy, relax under a red light, wear bright red shades, or hold a red object. Your hands are among the most powerful parts of your body in their ability to draw and to exude the magnetic current.

Use yellow for mental awareness. Moonlight, yellow flowers, yellow walls, all are useful in helping you to assimilate more knowledge, to use that which you already have.

For freshness, optimism, green is your color. Lie on grass, sit in a green-walled room, look at water.

You can use soft lavender if you seek tranquility. Because this is rare in your material world, lavender is not as easily found as other colors. Sometimes it is in the sky of a summer's evening, sometimes it is in the depths of a pool. You can always find it in the heart of a purple amethyst. Since summer evenings, still pools and amethysts are not always available, you can contemplate a flower or hold some soft material in your hands.

For a calm, detached attitude, use gray. This is the in-between color, the color of space between the physical and the real, the waiting color of anticipation without impatience. Wear gray, look at a quiet sky, touch a gray-furred animal, sit in a gray chair.

For rising joy, heightened awareness, use orange. The sunlight, the sunrise are expressions of this beautiful color. Ripe fruit of the orange tree, the full-grown carrot, a goldfish, are manifestations of the sun's color.

If you need a new planting of control, strength, calm approach to a material problem, brown will have the greatest effect on your body. Contact the earth, contemplate a tree trunk, wear a brown garment. The richness of the planet-color will fill you with its lush strength.

Pure black will pour through you a power that overcomes distortion and contributes to your invincibility. It is not an "evil", "negative" color. How can it be? It is a natural manifestation and therefore God.

Pure white will draw response from your inner self, making more brilliant its reflection upon the surface, overwhelming with light the darkness of any unbalanced condition. If you can, surround yourself with it. If this is not to be arranged, touch white, wear it, look at it somehow. Even a little is enough.

There are happy colors and there are angry shades. In their pure, natural state all are beautiful and positive, but when humanity mixes the basic shades chaos often results. One who is exceedingly miserable in his personal life will produce through mixture a shade which is upsetting. One who is bitter toward the world will produce a shade which is drab, ugly. Only happy, well-adjusted individuals should attempt to imitate God's pure tones, for individual expression cannot be left out of anything, no matter how automatic the activity seems to be.

Your understanding, as it grows, will encounter and absorb shades beautiful beyond those of the mortal plane. Colors have always been what they are, however, and always will be. The improvements, the growing beauty are due to your own awakening, the development of your ability to see with a clearer vision.

The rainbows of your heavens are lovely to material eyes, but their true beauty is not apparent to the unawakened beholder. The rainbows are in their selves glorious beyond description but they are manifesting in a field of vibration set by man and are therefore muted in their physical expression.

There is no clash between colors except in the mind of the beholder or in the mixing of nature's true shades. In a field of flowers, God has combined red with orange, green with blue, and there is no clash. Put every color of the rainbow side by side and they are harmonious to each other. If you are a person with self-control, without fear of others, with poise, you can combine colors which are conventionally frowned upon because you are expressing something from within and you have the right to do so.

You cannot find a spot in your world where there is no color because it is a part of creation. You cannot turn from color by wearing black, despite scientific pronouncement that it is the absence of color. Black is a color, just as red or blue or yellow are colors. If you submitted any color to a microscopic examination, you would find it contained all other colors, because all are one. They are

interlocked, integrated, and it is only as material expressions for material eyes they become individualized, varied.

You contain colors and they contain you. When you
can accept, then understand what this means, you will
really love and make use of the wonderful things color
offers you. Because it is a habit of the human mind to
follow the lead of others, it is best if you remind yourself
not to accept generalization of color for your personal
guide. You cannot use God's marvelous shadings for your
best advantage if you do not take them for your individual
purposes.

God is color, of course. Since you are also God, when
you have learned to control your surface self and are
operating from inner direction, you will find your response to color has changed. You will appreciate every
color, and you will not have a constant favorite, loving all
impartially. You can be greatly encouraged when you are
past any definite dislike for any color or colors.

What is color? Why, it is simply love, delicious to the
eye, warming to the heart. It is the expression of infinity
on the surface plane, of wordless beauty in a world full
of words. It is stillness, peace; light, joy; calm, meditation; wisdom, knowledge; exaltation, ecstasy; awe, worship.

The specific purposes of color are as myriad, as varied,
as the purposes of any part of your world. Color is a comfort and a strength; an appreciation and a recognition;
a practical and a glorious guide toward understanding.

Color overwhelms with its sunrises and sunsets. It ex-
cites wonder with its rainbows, its auroras. It brings tranquility with its pastoral scenes, awe with its mighty dis-
plays of lightning and thunderclouds.

Color makes a background for every action, sets the scene for every event. It gives emphasis to living. Color causes surroundings to become more than they have been and helps individuals to awaken to what they are. Color is the strength of grass, the beauty of plant life, the grandeur of the skies. It is one more visible, feel-able proof of God.

To use its potential to the fullest, make your surroundings the colors harmonious to your own attitude. Wear the colors which offer your individual attractiveness most gracefully. Use the colors most suited to you for expression in all you do.

Like color, music is expressed throughout all of your universe and beyond. Every sound in existence is music of some kind, and everything in existence contains sound, so contains music.

In the heavens about your earth, invisible to your physical eyes, inaudible to your physical ears, there is a great chorus of praise, sung to the Maker of all things by millions of voices who are gathered in their knowing selves.

The sound swells as it moves closer to the Source, and as your understanding awakens you will hear this heavenly choir. It has been described many times in the past by individuals who were considered mentally unbalanced. "The singing of angels, indeed!" Anything beyond the commonplace is not tolerated by the ignorant, who do not realize their "commonplace" is not normal other than in their own small worlds.

Everyone who reaches awareness hears the music of the spheres. There are no words, but in the sound itself the adoration for God is fully expressed. When you hear

63

this music it will fill you in a way you could not be filled on the physical plane. You will feel the might of it, the throb of its rhythm, and you will join in the singing, becoming one with the music of love.

In the trilling of birds, the singing of the winds, the sighing of waters, the busy hum of insects, in all sounds of your physical world lives the music of eternity. Each individual thing is expressing music in its individual way. You, with the sounds you make, are expressing also. If you have misunderstood the pattern of creation and there is a lack of harmony within your own mind, the sounds you make will not be pleasing to the ears of others. If you have a harmony within your mind of which you are conscious, you will express yourself to the world with beauty.

There is a rhythm of growth in all things, a pattern which does not deviate. There is a rhythm of expression in all things and this too may be recognized by the alert.

Your skies are pulsating continuously, the earth pulsates as it spins through the spaces of your material universe, the stars throb in the night, the sun throbs by day. Everything has a pulsebeat and its rhythm is determined by the degree of power expressed in the individual person or thing.

Music is the rhythm of creation, the harmony in which eternal awareness has its being, the melody of its expression throughout material dimensions. You respond to music as you respond to every force of nature. You may not have learned to channel your responses, but your reactions follow the laws and are inevitable.

There is music for every mood, for every occasion, for every experience. In the background of your life there is always sound, and this is the music to which you move.

If you believe yourself to be tone-deaf and have so manifested in your physical being, it is only because some past experience has drawn a curtain over your memory and you do not recall when you could sing with the birds.

Cacophony is distorted music, just as hate is distorted love, greed is distorted generosity, and fear is distorted trust. The harsh sounds produced by those who wish to be "progressive" are caused by the individuals' lack of harmony in their minds, their lack of understanding toward God. Although it may be the mode to profess appreciation of unrelated sounds clashing against each other, you need not pretend a liking for it. Unless these discordancies appeal to a distorted spot in your mind, you have the right to withdraw from the collection of listeners who delude themselves when they assure each other this is music.

As in all things, there are many varieties of expression from which to choose music that will bring forth your greatest response. You may prefer the haunting magic of a violin to the stirring notes of a bugle. You may prefer the primitive beat of a drum to the delicate tune of a pipe. Whatever your appreciation may be, it is right for you more than any other. The best music for you will fill your physical being, uplift you and give you renewed awareness.

Upon the earth, music has many expressions. A lullaby sings a child to sleep, a marching song stirs men to feats of daring, a lilting tune brings forth song, a soft rhythm brings relaxation for listening. There is music by which to dance, music to which you would give voice, music to fit your every mood.

If a home is filled with love, with harmony, you are aware of this the moment you step inside. The atmosphere is filled with love and it is obvious to all who enter.

If a home contains unhappiness, bitterness, it repulses you as you enter, because the discordant notes emitted by those who live there are clashing against each other in the atmosphere about you.

Communities whose people live in peace and mutual respect offer an attractiveness to you as you enter the outer limits, because each solo-song has joined all the others in a symphony of peace.

Countries which have existed in freedom for many years, whose peoples are self-reliant, self-respecting individuals, give out such songs of happiness and gratitude they draw others like a magnet.

Music swells birds so full of joy they sing until their throats would seem near to bursting. It sets the trees to dancing irresistibly when it comes to them on the winds. It turns running waters to liquid delight and seas to thunderous ovations.

Music fills the day with so many sounds they would clash if all were not the same voice singing. It fills the night with notes not heard by day, notes proclaiming the beauty of darkness, of peace, rest.

Life would indeed be empty without music, as it would be empty without any one of the marvels with which God has filled your world. While color delights the eye, the obvious, music delights the ear, the unseen parts of the material being. The two are a completely harmonious blending of awareness, knowing.

Music expresses every wonderful facet of love. It is joy, laughter, excitement, peace, worship. It is in every

66

sound you hear, in every object upon your earth. It is the sound of God's voice, living notes of beauty for the ears of any who will listen.

Music swells upon the air in spring with the calls of mating, the unfoldment of new life. Music slowly hums its awareness in summer, when the trees hold themselves still under the power of the sun's rays to absorb its strength. Music strikes through the atmosphere in the fall when the world of nature rushes to complete its cycle before another sleep. Music sounds softly in the winter, as snow mantles the earth and the cold snaps an occasional note with energetic explosion, when the apparent ending is in truth a preparation for renewed expression.

How inexpressibly marvelous is love, God's Being! He gives all and asks nothing, for in giving he has no room for asking. He gives simple things, obvious things like breathing, daylight and moonlight, then goes on to giving friendship, understanding. He gives the beauty of nature, and goes on to giving an awareness that exalts beyond all things on and of the earth.

Beauty must be fully appreciated if it is to be useful to you. All of God's Being is beautiful beyond measure, of course. As an individualization of that Measureless Beauty, you can travel closer and closer to it in recognition.

Include color in every part of your plan for material living. Include music in every part of your physical awareness. *Recognize* both, and greater and greater beauty will be yours to know.

UNDERSTANDING, ATTITUDE, AWARENESS

All material things are expressing in the mortal dimension according to their individual degrees of understanding, which are the accumulations of their past experiences, their past lives.

You too express according to this pattern, so do not censure yourself for "inferior" attributes or admire yourself for "superior" attributes. While *you* are what you have always been, without ego, without self-consciousness, your surface person is the composite of your past physical personalities. These have, through their reactions to their experiences, created present situations. Your present personality in turn creates certain situations for another surface being to experience in future. This will go on and on, until you have achieved the goal of all creation, until your material reactions have become *aware* attitudes, until your physical being reflects *you* in its every part.

Have you been waiting all of your life for something to happen? Although you make daily physical efforts, have you thought that beyond these efforts lay a goal which could be accomplished only by whim of fate—through your being on whatever great wheel of chance operates for special things, for special considerations?

It is not so. Your present material self is the sum of your conscious awareness of truth, no more, no less. When you are expressing to the fullest degree of your understanding, being what you know how to be, nothing more is demanded, nothing more is expected of you in the great Plan of creation.

Understand this clearly, that you yourself may accept all things for what they are and not what you would wish them to be, that you may accept yourself for what it is and not what you think it should be.

By realization of God, of the eternal self within, by physically expressing your growing awareness, your material personality will become more and more the reflection of *you*. Whatever your personality is, whether it responds to inner prompting slowly or swiftly, accept it fully as God's expression so your thought processes will not be occupied with fault-finding.

If the door is shut against God-consciousness, it is human ignorance which holds it shut. An honest mind will not condemn the unknowing, will understand. This intelligence is present everywhere, but because it is so available, so easily found, it is ignored or overlooked by the too-straining searchers.

If a man can find no reason in his own mind for not taking from another, he is expressing what he understands. When his understanding grows so he realizes he is entitled only to what is given to him, he will steal no more.

If a man really thinks he can cheat his fellow beings in business during the week, then by attending church on Saturday or Sunday become pure and virtuous, he is expressing to the fullest degree of his understanding.

Knowing these are distortions of truth only because consciousness has not been fully awakened, the Supreme Intelligence, God, does not expect more of these men than they are capable of expressing. Regardless of how small the conscious awareness of God may be, it is far better to live according to that awareness than to strain toward a "higher" goal of behavior. Honesty is always better than deceit, and he who attempts to be what he is not deceives himself much more than he deceives others. He also causes himself to be miserable, because he is under a strain every moment of the labored effort he must make to pretend.

You only fool yourself if you pretend to be anything other than what you are. You can only make believe, and make believe cannot be played indefinitely. At some period in your lifetime you come face to face with your self. If you are honest, if your mind has been trained to face facts, you will not turn and run, to hide in pretense again. You will become in your human personality the expression of what your conscious self knows how to be.

The Eternal Intelligence understands your human self, understands whatever you do. The Eternal Intelligence, understanding, does not judge or expect anything. Understanding, it simply loves.

Since this is true of God, can you, his expression, do less and condemn yourself for seeming to be inferior? Can your mind demand of your physical being that it do other than it is prepared to do, be other than it is prepared to be? Can you do less than love your individual self as a manifestation of God?

You can overcome any tendencies toward mental criticisms by remembering there is no "more" or "less" by the standards of eternal life—no more or less importance, no more or less admirable qualities, no more or less love given. God is constant, unchanging, all-encompassing. The fluctuations, the different degrees of awareness of his qualities are distortions caused by a confused transmission through the conscious (physical) mind.

70

There is never need for despair, regardless of what your surface self has done in the past. What might seem disgraceful or degrading to the *un*-understanding of the mortal plane is completely understood in the knowing dimensions. It is not shameful to have distorted purity of motive, only unknowing. When you *know* God's love you cannot distort. Until then, however, your physical actions are liable to be confused. In the Creator's compassion there is total warmth toward you, full comprehension.

Wrap about you, then, your stained garments, you who have been stoned, and give your bruised heart into the hands of God. Through his ministering you will come to command the respect of your fellow man.

Raise your bowed head, then, you who have been shamed by ignorance. Look to your God that you may see by his Light and henceforth pass beyond any shame.

Stand tall and with dignity, then, you who have been set aside from your world by a mistaken action. Walk with your God that your step will not falter again and you may find your true place among the mortals.

In any lingering despair, in any clinging sorrow, in any remembered shame, look deep within and find God shining forth. He will dissolve, dispel anything of the physical world which has marked your mind with pain. Nothing others do can touch you unless your physical being takes the bruises, the damage, to itself. This too you can erase in the radiance of God's love.

Remember, you are never past hope in any lifetime, in any circumstance. You can never sink so low you cannot rise to the heights. You are never an individual who should be avoided by your fellow beings, nor is there anyone whose deeds should cause you to avoid him.

You are all you need to be if you will express what is natural, unforced, for you to express. You have all you need to own if you will become aware of the treasures within you.

Give your human self an opportunity to find its rightful place in the material world by freeing it of any chains which bind it—guilt, memories, regrets. Free it by recognition of self, by giving self full charge of your life. Since you do not stand completely still at any point in your existence, some action is always taking place. Stop unknowing activities at once and aware motion will begin immediately.

The search for understanding is a long and dreary way to the stubborn, the proud, the willful. It is no search at all for the humble, the eager and the trusting. There *is* no long journey to take—unless the mind wishes to make it long. There is *no* high mountain to climb—unless the human ego has built it. There is nothing between God and the physical being unless surface stubbornness has erected a barrier.

If you have read many books, listened to many teachers, you may have reached a point of complete bewilderment about the attainment of understanding, for each has probably offered a different pattern to follow.

Everyone with a desire to help his fellow man puts forth suggestions. Do not be misled or deceived by these varying, individual viewpoints. They are meant only to be inspirations for you in seeking your own way, springboards for your own leap into awareness.

Your search for understanding will not bring you confusion if you maintain balance. Truth is a simple thing, as so many wise, humble ones have said, so the discovery of truth is simple also.

Do not be afraid to step out, to try your wings that you may soar aloft in the direction your individual self prefers. When a bird first leaves the nest it must wobble along awkwardly. It takes many falls, but through persistence it learns the correct muscles to use, the proper maneuvers to make that it may fly high into the sky as its parents did before it.

Persistence and confidence in its ultimate achievement are the two qualities the young bird expresses. You too have persistence, or you would have given up your human struggles long ago. All you need is the mental recognition that you also have confidence in your ultimate achievement of complete awareness. The confidence is there, but often unrecognized because it has not been brought to your attention.

Like the young bird, you cannot achieve anything without making an attempt. This holds true whether you are striving toward something in the physical world or seeking to grow in the spiritual dimensions. No one and nothing can move while holding still, and it is far better for you to make a mistake (perform a distortion of truth) through trying something of which you are not certain than it is to stand and wonder for the rest of your life if you would have made a mistake should you have tried.

It is better to learn through doing than it is to remain ignorant through inactivity, dormancy. Be brave, fearless. You have nothing to lose. If you are seeking anything, materially or spiritually, with an honest heart, an open mind and an humble attitude, you cannot—you *can*

73

not fail. You *can not* go in the wrong direction and come up against disaster.

Being brave, fearless, means you are clinging without reservation to a complete faith in your Creator. That is all it amounts to, no more, no less, because faith brings you through any door, across any threshold, beyond any emptiness. The fearless ones of your planet are those who are happy, who are serene, without worries, without cares of any kind. They do not concern themselves with the food their stomachs will need at the next meal. They do not concern themselves with where they will next lay their heads in sleep, or with what garments they may cover their nakedness. They know all of this is a part of living, of being cared for and protected.

They know there is *plenty* for all upon your planet. Despite statistics which indicate the growing population soon will reach such proportions the earth cannot produce the food to sustain it, there *is* plenty. In the expression of the natural laws of creation, more foods are produced. As each individual expresses that which he was intended to express, he himself produces the condition and the supply for every need he could have, and beyond.

To realize this for yourself, you have only to let go of fear, of doubt, of despair. Let go, and jump in some direction. Close your eyes if you must, if you are not sure, but jump. This you must do if you are to move from the spot upon which you are standing, if you are to climb out from any rut in which you have been trapped, if you are to open for yourself the wide, beautiful vistas which are yours rightfully.

You cannot be miserable unless your mind is full of self-criticism and uncertainty. Your mind cannot fail to be happy if you are full of faith, and when you enjoy living each day and each night, the world about you is a marvelous and a lovely place.

Fill yourself with the cup that overflows. This is the belief that makes you joyous every moment. You cannot keep laughter from your lips, love from your heart when you have faith. Is this not a wondrous thing, this trust to which you can cling in any situation, during any period of time, in any location, for any purpose?

Express faith and you will immediately see the results. Live with faith and you will *truly* live instead of merely existing in a cocoon of ignorance. Have faith, and wisdom will open to you as a flower opens to the sunlight. Have faith, give love, because in the giving you are expressing God, and when you have faith you glow with love.

Faith brings awareness, which is the knowing of God's presence. How this awareness manifests on the material plane is not of any importance whatsoever. You are free to live as you see fit, to worship as you wish. You have only two things to remember, really, in your seeking: One, in order to find complete happiness with your destiny, complete acceptance of God, you need a faith right for you whether or not it is right for anyone else; two, you must allow all others their individual faiths no matter what they may be, no matter how close those individuals are to you in surface relationship.

Faith brings understanding, which encompasses your acceptance that others should not seek your expression, and that you should not seek theirs. Understanding includes *acceptance,* not tolerance, that the surface differences of the world are only varied expressions of the one Power. Understanding gives the *knowing* of God.

If you would conquer material life, keep it at your command, never say, do not even think, "I will try." You will have defeated your purpose before you begin making any effort. You cannot finish anything, you cannot accomplish, if you only *try*. You must *do it*. This is faith expressed in action.

If your mind has an attitude of just trying, it has accepted defeat before it begins. If your mind is trained to consider only the ultimate accomplishment, to trust fully in the power of God, its attitude will allow no room for anything except achievement. Everything in your life is dependent solely on your attitude. If you expect only the best of results from your efforts you will meet with success, because you have faith in the law of balance. If you expect only love from those you encounter, you will meet friendship and admiration because you have faith in the law of love. *Whatever you expect you get,* and your expectation in any situation is your *attitude,* the degree of your trust.

You have probably thought at times in the past that you get anything except what you expect, because you have tried to accomplish something you did not accomplish, have offered a friendship that was rebuffed, or have prayed for some favor you did not receive. Friend, if you had not *expected* these defeats you would not have had them! You alone are the open door to your success or the barrier which causes your defeat.

If your "faith" is that of the individual who prays for rain, then when it does not come says, "Humph! I knew all the time it wouldn't rain!", you have expressed a defeated expectancy and that is exactly what you get—a defeated result. You have believed in failure rather than

76

accomplishment, no matter how insistently your mind declares this is not so.

Your Bible says, "Ask and ye shall receive." It does *not* say, "If God is in the right mood today," or "If what you ask is good for you." It makes a firm statement of fact, too often overlooked in the search for an excuse to explain why a request is not granted. You *do* receive exactly what you ask (expect), for it is your attitude, the extent of your faith, which creates each experience you have in your life, whether it is personal or impersonal, material or spiritual.

If you are not a business success today it is because you have not truly expected to be one, although you may have spent years trying, you may have toiled long hours every day. Nevertheless, you did not expect to succeed, you did not believe you could, or you would have done so. This explains why so often the individual who seems to have made very little effort is an overnight success while another has labored all of his life and still does not accomplish anything materially. Even if this individual's past experiences have produced his present success, those past experiences must have contained the expectation of succeeding. Physical effort is *not* the expression of faith; *attitude* is.

If you are lonely, completely without friends, it must be that you do not expect others to like you or to find you interesting. You must not believe God has given you everything he has to give. When you walk into a roomful of people with the attitude, "No one will notice me", you have created an invisible wall—disbelief—which will effectively bar any interest you might have aroused otherwise.

It may be well to remind you here that no criticism is ever implied or intended in truth. Truth is a statement of fact, not a fault-finding personal reaction. Truth is an effort to lighten the darkness and so show the path that you may step with confidence upon it, choosing your own direction and the length of your stride. Criticism is a cruelty in any case, and certainly has no place at the side of love, where you will find truth, trust. If you have held yourself back from happiness in the material world, it is because you did not understand and therefore did not trust; did not realize God's all-mightiness and therefore did not have faith.

The human body and mind without the guidance of the Eternal Intelligence are similar to an automobile without a driver. *You* must manipulate the gears, *you* must turn the motor, *you* must regulate the speed. Like a child who misbehaves, your mind also is not bad, only unknowing. As you train it, your mind will grow, will operate exactly as directed so you will find the results manifesting in your life with happiness and fulfillment in your days. Until that "education" is accomplished, your not knowing could hardly be reason for censuring you.

Attitude marks one individual from another. He who expects to win defeats him who expects to lose. Both may have said they would win, but their *attitudes* were not the same. One may have said he would win but in his own mind actually expected to lose, so he does. The other has faith in his own physical ability because he also has faith in God's power to express through his material self. He may not think such a thought consciously, but he has that attitude nevertheless.

There is no such thing as being refused that which you ask (expect), not finding (realizing) that which you seek (open to). You get what you ask for, you find what you seek. You have only to know (accept) what you are asking, to know (understand) what you are seeking. You have only to believe in your Creator's ability, to trust your inner self.

You must learn how to ignore the comments of your mind, the whims of your material being, for these are as the wind, moving constantly and shifting as they go. Can you not remember a situation such as this? You think you want something. You want it so much that you are unhappy that you do not have it. You say a prayer, make a declaration, are filled with wishful thinking. Whatever your method, you do not get what you want, and you wonder why. The next day, or in a few days, you want something else and the process begins all over.

If this has been your experience, you have allowed your material mind to express its whims freely. Because of long-established habit, it has been aimless in its action, weak in its attempts. What if you truly wanted something? What if you *knew* it was right for you? If your attitude was one of acceptance, of faith that it would be yours, the way would open for your attaining it. Why? Because you would have put into action the irresistible power of *right attitude,* faith.

Some desires may seem unimportant in comparison to the major needs of your physical self, but there is no such thing as unimportance in the scheme of creation, and your urges toward certain things are as much the result of past activity as your other material expressions. Everything you accomplish materially is important, wheth-

79

er it is an heroic deed or the tying of a shoelace. Each thing you do is *you* expressing in action, and each action is taking you further along the way to fulfillment.

The law of cause and effect, of balance, is the law behind your attitude. Fear God, and you cannot get past that fear, but give God your unquestioning trust and you will consciously receive his constant protection. Give him your love and you will be made aware of his divine love.

Today, *now*, ask what you will as long as it is a sincere, undistorted request, expecting to get it, and your wish will be fulfilled. Test the truth of this statement. Make it prove itself to you. Seek with the attitude, the expectation of finding your goal. You will not be disappointed. You are asking your eternal self to act, opening the way for it by believing it can and will produce anything your surface being requires.

That great one *you* are in reality will answer your every true call, will fill your every true need and longing, when your conscious mind expresses happy anticipation, complete trust, living faith.

You are on the threshold of unfoldment every moment, any second, of your physical existence. At any instant you can take the one short step into the realms of fulfillment. The truth, being close and of easy access, is usually overlooked in the common search for complication. Your eyes will miss the beautiful bird sitting on the tree bough close above your head if they are focused on a faraway star. Your ears will miss his lovely song if they are listening too intently for the words of other human beings.

If you sincerely yearn to know the pure formula of life, the way to express your faith at once, without elaborate preparation or training; if you humbly look with open, eager mind for understanding that you may be the physical expression God planned you to be, the secret is available for your enlightenment. Unless you are still doubtful of God's might and of your ability to reflect it, you have no need for a book filled with detailed instructions, no need for a series of lectures or a study course of lessons.

If you want a shortcut because you are ready to be whatever God's bidding may be, if you want truth in a capsule, here it is: Become, BE *aware*.

In this great maelstrom of ignorance which is your world, all you need is awareness. Give God, any God you accept, your attention. Constantly feel the love from within pouring forth to become one with That which created your conscious person. Express your trust in all phases of your physical life, no matter what they seem to be.

You can do almost nothing physically or you can labor all day and far into the night. You can serve others or be withdrawn from the world. You can travel the seven seas or live your span in one room. None of these things are of any importance. All you need, all that is required of you for completion is *awareness*. All that matters on the mortal plane is *what* you express, not *how* you express it.

If your present conscious mind cannot let go, cannot become the transmitting unit it is intended to be and prefers a long, devious route, it is your privilege to travel toward understanding via every detour your physical self can find.

If you prefer a labored, slow journey toward understanding by shutting off the self who tries to enlighten

81

you and turning to other individuals, it is your privilege to sit at the feet of the equally unawakened.

You, like all other expressions of God, will inevitably reach the goal of truth, of awareness. Slow or swift, easy or difficult, your journey is in that direction. You will arrive at your destination, and will find there before you the one who trusted the self within.

Inevitably, you will come to a place on your pathway where the signpost is clearly marked for your mind. It reads, "Alone from this point on". When you arrive at this sign and read its directions, your mind will never again think it requires anyone or anything outside of *you* to take you into the Creator.

Be aware of the closeness of God to your conscious being, that it may express unwavering faith and find fulfillment instantly.

Understand the laws of creation and awaken your surface to the realization that you truly are loved. After all, *understanding* is simply loving, and loving is the expression of self, of *you*.

Bless you, and may awareness, faith, understanding be yours forever, from this moment onward. Bless you, beloved. May your back be unbound and your step light.

LET YOUR SELF GO

If you had no more goals to strive toward, if you had no more knowledge to learn, if you had no more understanding to seek, your life would become pointless, meaningless, empty. Be grateful, therefore, that you do not have all you want in the material world, that you are still unknowing of all wisdom beyond the physical plane, as long as you are not yet fully aware. Be grateful that when you have reached a longed-for point in your life there is at once another point you wish to reach.

Without learning the inner being which is you in truth, you cannot hope to come to an understanding of your own life and thence to a balance for your physical days. If you do not know your true self, how can you realize what is out of focus with your surface self? How can you find why your steps have always seemed to go in the wrong direction, and your words have always been lost in unimportance to others?

The only time to plan on creating new conditions in your life is *now*. If you put your plans off and do not give them your attention until tomorrow or next week or next year, you will find the day has not come when you are ready to contemplate and then to put into action your blueprint for living. Tomorrow does not arrive and there is only now in which to plan your steps toward self-understanding, self-acceptance, and therefore contentment, toward being your self, being *you*.

It is the striving, the effort which keeps you moving, whether you are heading toward a material or a spiritual goal. Of course, those aware ones who have an understanding of God are not striving or seeking, but these have found the great goal of *be*-ing. Only a few expressing on the mortal plane have reached this degree of awareness. The rest must be made aware on the conscious level of the pressure from within, must keep going until they too eventually know the constant peace of full awareness.

You as an individual must express in your own unique fashion to be completely happy as a human being. Although the inner you is a part of the creation and therefore identical to, one with, all other parts, the personality through which that inner being expresses is different and must express differently. It is a fallacy to believe you can find happiness or success or any of the things you seek through imitation of others, through accepting the words of others and following them, simply because these other individuals have found their paths and wish to pass their ways to you.

How can any other tell you exactly what you should do and when to do it, when only you have experienced the many things which have come into your atmosphere through many lifetimes? There can be no predetermined reaction to any situation because your reaction will be based upon past experience, and your experience is not the same as any other's.

Your inner self—*you*—must be applying pressure for an opening through which to express or you would not be making any effort toward self understanding, understanding of God. This is not the pressure, the force, of distorted, would-be conquest but the power of the inner being's magnetic current pushing against its confinement. Like any natural part of creation, its power can be contained only for a certain period, then the pressure of the vital necessity for expression becomes overwhelming.

This is why an individual who has been a model of deportment sometimes suddenly goes berserk. The surface being has not allowed itself to express naturally, but has adhered to all of the rules and regulations of society, of convention. When the true being has been stifled to a point where there is no more room for it to be imprisoned, its power breaks loose. The individual's surface being, conditioned to distortion, reacts by an ignorant action and unhappiness is the result.

The honor student who has never given his parents or his teachers any trouble, who gets along well with his schoolmates, suddenly goes mad and kills a smaller child. His explanation almost invariably is, "Something *made* me do it. I couldn't help myself."

The adult who has lived circumspectly all of his life, who has allowed others to treat him with condescension and discourtesy, suddenly turns on his wife or some person in authority over him and slays. When confronted with his deed, he almost always says something like, "I don't know why I did it. Suddenly I couldn't stand it any more." When asked what "it" is, he does not have a coherent answer.

Why do such things happen? Because repression of self-expression is a definite act of upsetting an individual's equilibrium, and another expression must take place to follow the law of balance. Why do acts of violence follow apparently complete virtue? Because the conventional rules of behavior in the so-called advanced parts of the world are unnatural, unbalanced, and so contribute to individual repression.

You are not being advised that society's laws should be flouted at every opportunity. You are not being told to do everything oppositely to the laws of your civilization. You *are* being told that any regulation set upon itself by society, by civilization, which goes contrary to your *natural* inclinations is artificial and therefore is not good for you. Repression of yourself will cause far more damage to the surface being than the greatest material hardship, the most extreme mental pressure. You cannot be any of the things God intended you to be unless you reflect your God-self as an individual, and for the most part, the world would make you into an identical expression of everyone else.

At this point, this may sound like a very dangerous statement indeed. What of those individuals who release their inclinations by robbing others, by committing violence upon others? As with every fact, you must know *all* of it to understand it. Expression of self is at no time a distorted process. Since self is God, there can be only right impulse from it. Any action which is not correct is therefore not a true expression of the inner being.

If expression of self is positive, why does the student who has been good go berserk, and why does the man who has always been virtuous suddenly become violent?

Turn to the rules of convention, the laws of society. The boy who does not once disobey his parents is *not* expressing his individual *self*. No parent, being human, can be correct always in knowing what is best for a child. The child's instinct, much stronger than that of an adult, tells him what is correct or mistaken for him individually. For this reason, the ideal relationship between parents and child is one of cooperation, mutual respect, understanding, love. No healthy, well-adjusted child will give his parents total, unquestioning obedience, because this is in direct opposition to the God-established instinct for individual freedom.

The man who has been a "good" boy, who has no "bad" habits, never talks back to anyone, speaks up in his own defense or expresses an opinion is trying to make believe he is not alive at all. He *cannot* express self by complete effacement of his surface personality. He is doing the one thing which insures any human being total misery—he is denying his birthright to be free and individual, he is not being honest with himself.

Because he is a human being, because he is not of the aware who cannot be touched by the things of the world, he must have, many times, wanted to lash out at his tormentors, to answer those who took advantage of his servile attitude. Yes, servile. The man who does not figuratively look the world in the eye is a servile, kneeling individual. Since he was born with the right to be himself, he is blasting his own well-being by refusing to allow his self or his human person any expression at all. By subduing his inner being he creates surface distortions, ignorant impulses, and these too he subdues until they cannot be controlled by his physical mind any longer.

No one except the great beings can experience a physical life without the desire to express as a surface person. Until you can be opened in your material being to full freedom for your eternal self, you will no doubt have many inclinations which are only whims of your material person. Remember, because you are a human being you are intended to express as such, not as anything else, so human traits are expected of you. They are not judged wicked or unnatural by any eternal intelligence.

Some individuals misunderstand this and have decided that perfection in God's eyes can only be reached by the complete suppression of every natural instinct, by complete denial of every normal inclination. If their ideas are correct, why do they not become "perfect" in every physical way, why are they not totally happy? Why, when they deny every part of their human selves, do they not reach the perfection which they claim is the attainment made through self-denial?

Why? Because they are expressing as they *think* they should instead of as they *feel* they want to. God gave every individual thing every attribute it has. This includes the physical mind and body of the human being. He gave all things his free will, he gave all things the awareness within them. Since God is all there has ever been, he gave of himself also when he created the organs of the body, the appetites of the human body, just as he gave of himself in creating the bodies of all things.

Any part of God, when over-used or suppressed to an extreme by material ignorance, is a distortion of truth, a false reflection of this God in the surface dimension. Those who indulge themselves in activities of the mortal plane must learn to balance through the realization their indulgences are a form of sickness, and the only way to healthy living *is* balance. Those who suppress themselves will find their way to balance through the same results, for no matter which extreme of anything is practiced, the results are alike.

Too much food causes discomfort and illness. Not enough food produces the same condition. Too much recreation without any work weakens the physical strength and results in boredom. Too much work without any relaxation produces the same result. Too much sexual activity without love results in debilitation. Complete repression of any natural sex impulse produces the same result.

You have, perhaps, been conditioned to think of plenty in terms of a table groaning under its load of food. You may have been trained to work hard for your living almost every waking moment because that is supposed to be the only way you can get anything you want. You may have been taught that the desire for oneness on the material plane is a shameful desire, that procreation is the only right motive for the act of copulation; or that you may know others in casual intimacy without feeling more than the wish to indulge surface appetites.

If so, are you happy with this training, any of this teaching? Are you comfortable when you have so filled your stomach with food it hurts and you are so heavy you cannot move? You would not continue to pour fuel into a motor after its tank was filled. Food is put into the body to keep it active, in good condition. You waste supply deliberately if you eat more than you need. You are actually destroying the health of your own body bit by bit when you force it to handle more than nature equipped it to dispose of.

If you are starving your physical self, are you calm and serene? Are you happy, alert, vivacious? Your body must have food to operate, just as any machine must have fuel to keep running.

Are you contented with laboring every waking moment when you are not eating? Do you feel a joy within you as you work, or are you aware of a hopelessness, a despair, in your mind? One of God's expressions through you is joy, laughter. You cannot be filled with laughter if you labor all of your days.

Neither can you be joyous for long if you only play. Work and play are the two parts which equal the balance. You must have some of both to be happy. Unless you are being useful in some way to someone, you are not being of any use to yourself.

Are you complete without the intimate knowing of another? Do you feel no void in your heart as you ignore the love your own being tries to express? What is so shameful about physical love that it must be suppressed, reviled or completely ignored? You find nothing shameful about eating, drinking, sleeping. You find nothing shameful in speaking or in moving about. These are natural expressions, natural to your physical body.

Believe this: There is never anything shameful in any part of the expression of love, for each is God's action and each has its place in your destiny. If it is not in your pattern for this lifetime to know another in intimacy, your expressions of love will follow other channels. But if you are to meet the personal love of another individual, take that love gladly and give yours freely. You will be experiencing the oneness of completion, the acme of exalted oneness in the world of mortals.

Over-indulgence in sexual activity brings a deadly attitude of boredom toward the opposite sex, a weakening of the physical condition, a mental state of disinterest in life. Love is meant to be given freely, but this is not an indication that physical actions are always performed in the name of love. *Feeling* from the most sacred, innermost self is given in the moments of oneness if love is being expressed. Self-satisfaction, *taking* from another is only distortion masquerading as natural instinct, selfishness robbing the deluded one of life's greatest gift, love.

In every part of the material planet there are two— the male and the female; the right and the left; the up and the down; the give and the receive; the day and the night. To balance anything there must be two parts, for it is the exact center of these two parts, their meeting-place, which is the balance. When a man and a woman are one in love, they are completed, balanced. They are the surface reflection, the physical expression of the oneness, the completion, the allness of God.

Unless some past experience has drawn the curtain across your individual inclination, you will have healthy appetites toward all parts of your physical world. If you suppress these completely your material self will be sick with frustration. If you saturate your appetites to extremes, your material being will be ill also, because you will have passed your physical capacity.

If you will let go of any past training, teaching, conditioning, and will live naturally, you will be a happy, well-adjusted individual. You will enjoy some activities more than others, and these are the activities for you. This statement can be made freely because the *natural* expression of self, remember, is the intent of God. When following your own instinct for expression you will be walking the path you are meant to walk, learning the lessons you are supposed to learn. You need have no fear the expression of self will be distorted if you truly follow your *self* promptings and not your *mind's* inclinations.

When you seek within yourself in the adventure toward

understanding, you do not duplicate the actions of anyone else. It is so important that you understand you cannot place your feet in the footprints of others. You cannot lead the way for anyone else. You must go your own way, and whether your own way will lead you through activities which are a part of the world you have known materially or whether they are beyond in the great unknown, you must follow these activities freely and without fear if you would come to your realization.

Violence is the result of unknowing attitude somewhere, sometime. It is *not* an expression of self, but distortion of an inner compulsion. Confine a creature who has always been free, and the longer it is confined the wilder it becomes. The *power* of its inner urge to express does not change or lessen, so the more its freedom is curtailed the stronger grows the backlog of the current of power. No one and no thing can be confined indefinitely without disastrous results. If you are any less than well-adjusted and happy, *now* is the time to begin freeing yourself of the inhibitions of false standards.

Lip service to anything has never made it ruler in actuality. Society preaches one thing and practices another. Individuals profess to follow one set of standards and live by another. Do not allow these facts to escape your attention any longer. *You* know the only standard perfect for your physical self to follow. *You* know the only rules perfect for your material self to obey. The perfect standards and rules for *you* to express through your surface being are completely positive, with no loopholes for distortion, so do not hesitate to adhere to them.

When you have learned to still the physical individual and have been in the silence so peace has filled your be-

ing, you will find your sense of values is changing. You will
find your attitude in general is changing, and you will
find you are becoming more aware of the things upon
the material plane than you have ever been before. You
will look at God's handiwork and this time you will look
and *see*. You will feel your physical body absorbing an
appreciation, a wonder at the diversity of the things which
have been caused to exist upon the material plane. You
will appreciate beauty far more than you have in the
past, before complete awareness was awakened.

It is a habit with the human being of today to go about
his business with his mind set fast upon one fact—where
he is going, or what he is doing—, and all other matters
are unnoticed, ignored. The wonders of the world, the
fact that this individual body is full of light and has all
of the material world before his feet will be completely
overlooked by the unknowing. But when you are aware,
you will take the time to pay homage to those things of
the physical world which have been made to express so
they and you could operate in perfect harmony, reflect
the perfect love which is the Creator.

You cannot learn all there is to know in a lifetime or
in many lifetimes. Because God is all there is, all powerful, without boundaries, the knowledge of God must be
the same. No one can know all of everything until he
ceases to be an individual expression. What you are doing now is taking a small step in the direction of understanding.

The human mind puts any limitation upon the love received and the love expressed in the material world. This
is the limitation which exists in the physical plane alone,
the make-believe limitation without reality, the only

limitation: the human mind. When you have disciplined your mind you will have no further adversaries, no more battles, no more mountains to climb or rivers to cross.

When you have been practicing for some time the awareness that you are a part of creation which is equal in importance to all other parts, and have acknowledged that which is within you is a self indestructible and eternal, you will have reached a point of readiness. Now you should be able to shed all of the everyday matters which ordinarily plague the human brain, and go into the realms of knowing which you seek in some manner, regardless of your station in life, your occupation, or your religious convictions.

You must understand that religion as it is practiced upon the surface has no connection with your real faith, your inner expression, beyond the fact that it is your material reflection of the inner you, constantly seeking to realign itself with God, because it was God who put himself in your spot and said, "Let this be a human being," and so it was. The human being is *you* expressing through your physical self, it is the reflection of *you*. Your religion is the surface expression of your inner awareness of God.

You have probably lived most of your life with a complex, a complex which caused you to believe you were less than others in many ways and perhaps in all ways. This inferiority can not be fact. A God which is everything and is impartial and impersonal in his love does not choose you above all others or others above you. He cannot, for he would be choosing himself over himself, a useless, senseless action.

If you cross a street, you go from one side to the other of your own volition, you are the one who propels yourself across. No one lifts you up and carries you over, pushes or pulls you. So it goes with all phases of your existence. What you yourself do produces another action you will encounter, and that next action will produce another after that. You are now expressing the results of past actions and you are setting the stage for future actions with your degree of conscious awareness of truth.

You—you alone—place your feet upon the path of enlightenment. You do not go backward at any time, no matter how much you might ignore the truths of creation, but you can keep yourself at an almost complete stand-still physically, moving at a snail's pace through the years, when you could be flying toward fulfillment. In these periods you will find your greatest despair without understanding the reason for it.

You have many needs within your surface being, only one of which is to learn self-acceptance and self-understanding. Beyond this you no doubt have a desire to *do* something, for it is a human urge to be active and it is caused by the *inner* urge to push forward steadily and constantly toward the point of fulfillment which will be yours eventually, inevitably.

No one knows how long, how many lifetimes, it will take for you to find your way back to the Source of all things. It might be you are very close to returning to that current of oneness. It might be you have a long journey to travel. No one can say to you that you are further along the path, or that you lag behind on the road to that understanding which carries an individual beyond any earthly condition and into the ecstasy of knowingness.

Your urge to action is understandable and of course it is necessary until you can *be* with full awareness of what *you* are. You, as a surface being, would not strive to exist upon the earth if you did not have this urge. You would not care to learn beyond that which is necessary for providing the material wants for yourself if you did not have it.

Your central intelligence, which does not die, which does not pause in any dimension at any time, can direct your physical intelligence, your mind, so you can win the struggle which goes on constantly in your brain. The human mind, as you know, is a willful thing. If it is worthwhile to you to lose all of the unhappiness you have known and to find all of the joys you have longed for, then turn your life over to that intelligence. Let it tell you what to do.

Apply your understanding to your everyday life now. You are ready to activate some of the knowledge you have discovered, to express it upon the surface. Do not let the thought of any possible changes in your life frighten you, for life itself is a constant change. Each day is a series of changes, and each night brings changes also, so in the morning when you arise the world is different and you are different in your surface person. All things are growing, every second. You too grow, and the direction of your growth is up to you.

How shall you apply what you have learned? Like all other parts of truth, this is very simple. You need only make an effort to remind yourself to do it, because the doing itself comes effortlessly.

If you have really learned relaxation, you can apply this to your activities during the day. You will no longer save the ability to relax for those periods when you can be alone, but whenever you feel the need for a moment's pause, whenever you feel a physical tension coming upon you. You will take a deep breath, and as you let it out your body *will* relax completely, regardless of where you are or what you are doing. You may be standing or sitting, you may be speaking before a large audience or working alone. It does not matter, because all you are doing is easing the tension of the various parts of your body. You are not going into meditation; you are simply causing your material body to relax so it can function as it was meant to function. It cannot operate correctly if it is tense, bound by static conditions.

When your mind is filled with a problem and you cannot seem to solve that problem, or if you have a decision to make and it is too much for you to handle, you will ease your mind. You will deliberately withdraw it from that which is worrying you, occupy it with whatever is of relaxation to you, and then calmly and casually allow the answer to anything you need to come into your mind quickly, without fuss. You will find you truly work these miracles with instant success once you have learned the process for doing so is easy and natural.

Prove these things for yourself. Prove that your body can be relaxed at once, no matter where you are or what you are doing, by taking a deep breath and, as you let it out, holding in your mind the fact that your body *is* relaxed completely. This takes only seconds, and you can go on with what you are doing almost without a pause. Test the fact that the relaxation of your mind can help you in the functioning of that same mind; that you can, by deliberately removing or letting go of anything which disturbs you mentally, conquer it, solve it, and go on as if you had not been troubled at all.

These are material actions by which you can not only express what you have learned, but you can prove anew to your surface self that everything in truth *can* be reflected upon the physical plane with ease once you have learned what it is you are doing and the habit of doing it.—Not the *how* of accomplishment, but the things you can do to *start* the accomplishment will be your training. Let creation itself take care of the how's. You are simply to know that you are doing your part in opening the way to that accomplishment.

In applying the simple rules of relaxation to everything you do physically, you will find your way is eased in the world about you, for only those who are relaxed can conquer in the true, right way. Those who seem not to care whether they win or lose, who seem indifferent because they are so relaxed they are not thinking of any competition in itself but only of the joy they have in doing what they are doing, are destined to win, for their relaxation is the attitude of the triumphant.

There is room for every material expression of God to triumph in every way over the material atmosphere in which he or it has being. This applies to work, to play, to contact with your fellow beings, to every part of your planet. Learn to live with relaxation and you have learned a very important, necessary way of walking another step toward the contact with the magnetic current, taking you anywhere you wish to go materially, and toward the eternal realms beyond your material dimension where true fulfillment awaits you.

You do not need to announce aloud you will follow only your self from now on. You do not need to confide in anyone that you have released the fears, the chains and the artificialities of empty words from surface standards. Your only need to remember is that *you* do not make mistakes, *you* are always perfect, *you* are following the laws of God because *you* are the laws of God. Your mind will learn that God's laws do not disagree with each other in any way at any time, while the laws of man are constantly clashing. Your mind will learn that living by the Creator's laws produces harmony so great there is not even any disharmony, discord, with surface regulations.

If it is shameful to some that anyone should advocate natural living, free expression of God, with a relaxed attitude toward all things at all times, loyalty to the inner self instead of the outer opinions of others, let those be shamed who will. Not the knowing ones, not you, beloved one, when you fully understand that in living by creation's standards you do harm to none, you stand in the way of none, you force none, you wrong none.

Open your surface being and let your self go, to express laughter, happiness, love in the material world *now*.

If this is revolt, so be it!

MEDITATION

After you have found your solitude and are able to be open to it, the time will come when your awareness of being, of the great love, light and warmth within and about you becomes so great your body will react with a physical "letting go."

Rejoice when your first moment of complete release comes to you, because it will be a sure indication you have found the state of consciousness which is the culmination of the search within the human individual for awareness.

Your material body is operating according to a certain rate of vibration. Each individual—person and thing —in the physical world has an individual vibratory action, and this is slow or fast, weak or powerful, according to the particular expression, to the particular milestone each thing has reached in understanding.

Your field of vibration, if you have only recently begun your movement toward awareness, will have been much less powerful than it will when you have awakened to and can maintain that awareness. When the magnetic current first touches you, it will be with only a small quantity of power, but your body will feel as if it had received a slight shock; not a painful one, but a tingling, rather startling sensation. As you develop in your meditations, your physical rate of vibration, the power of the current in you will increase until eventually you will be transmitting the magnetic current at such a strong rate it can make itself felt in other individuals. You will become like a battery full of power, and when this happens you will find you are becoming more and more physically fit in every way. More than that, you will find you are becoming a channel for the healing power of God to touch others. Eventually, perhaps very soon, you will be able to receive, maintain and transmit so much of the magnetic current it will crackle from your fingertips visibly.

Every experience you encounter, every reaction you feel in your solitude cannot be described or recognized here, but certain ones may be pointed out that you can be prepared to understand them as they come to you, that you may know all of your experiences are wonderful, whether you understand them at the moment or not, and all of your reactions will be nothing more than your physical body's expression of the activities of the inner self, as your physical mind understands those activities.

The moment may come very soon after you have begun your meditations when you are released completely from your material self or it may not come until many months have passed. There is no way of saying when a new door will open to you, because as an individual you will react in your own manner to each opening. However, there are certain things which, in a general sense, are experienced by most people who sit in meditation. These things are not identical, but are similar in their expressions. The release is one of these, and when you have finished your meditation, in this release you will know the exalted, life-giving quality which you can find only in your deepest moments alone with God. You are so revived after such an experience, so rejuvenated, you will feel as if you had been given renewed life itself.

There is no fatigue caused when you become aware of your God. If you are tired, exhausted, after having been still for a period, it is because you have been forcing with your mind, attempting to push action which will come to you rightfully without mental strain. Any conscious effort will tire your physical being so it will be weakened for a time. If this should happen to you, be very sure in your next meditation that you do nothing more than keep your body relaxed, your mind still.

You do not need to hurry. You have all the time there is. Even if you are ninety-nine years old, you have lots of time. The urge to rushing is a physical expression of the pressure to be doing something, going somewhere. In sitting still, remember *you* are accomplishing, so there is no need to make a material effort of any kind.

In your solitude, as you become aware of things beyond the room in which you sit with your eyes shut, beyond the world you have known, you may "see" clouds, blue sky, endless space, a foglike substance, a beautiful scene. Whatever you see, it will give to you a building of confidence, it will give you encouragement to continue your solitary meditations. The difference between this seeing and the projection of your conscious mind is that the latter is a deliberate extension of your mental activities and the former is an involuntary experience of your inner consciousness.

You may experience a sensation that you have suddenly become a balloon about to take off from its moorings and soar into the stratosphere. You might, rather than this, have a feeling you are a balloon *expanding* beyond your physical body, or you might feel you are a balloon *separating* from your physical body.

None of these need give you the least apprehension or cause for the slightest hesitation before letting go with your mind and allowing your true being to do what it will, because this *is* your true being. The sensation of having become a balloon is due to the sudden lightening of your self when it is freed from the human anchor of your physical body. When you feel you are going to soar, it is because *you* are ready to rejoin the spaces of creation with surface consciousness of your activities.

If you feel you are expanding so much your mind is almost afraid you will explode, be grateful you are experiencing this sensation, because it means *you* are expanding beyond the physical plane into the endlessness of creation, where you can again be all things with realization. If you have the sensation of separation, be grateful for this, because it is the release of your true being, stepping aside to express itself in freedom, moving about in another plane of awareness.

You may not understand the following words, but please keep your mind open to them for now. Within the room where you have your material being, there is more than one plane of expression, and it is only because you cannot see with your physical eyes or be aware with your physical mind as yet that prevents these planes from becoming known to you. They are real, as are the endless dimensions of any part of creation.

You may approach a vortex, once you have released your being from the confines of your material body. You may enter the outer edges of this vortex, begin to go around and around with it, and be stricken with fear that you will become dizzy, that you will remain there, whirling forever, or that you will be taken into some horrible motion, some horrible experience, with which you cannot cope. This too is all part of reality, so go into it with a great joy and an eagerness. If you follow the vortex, let yourself go with it, you will pass through it and come out at the other end, finding you are in a dimension of the awareness you have been seeking.

Perhaps instead of a vortex you will go through a tunnel. You may pass through it upon your hands and knees or standing erect, or you may go through without any consciousness of movement, for movement as you have known it is another part of the material plane. Whether vortex or tunnel, whether holes, doorways, or some other type of opening, you are seeing in manifestation the action of transference from the material plane to the plane of expression which draws your eternal being.

Go gladly, go without hesitation, for *you* will return to merge again with your physical body when the moment is right that you should do so. There is no danger whatsoever in doing this, because God is doing it. The only arrangement it is wise to make before meditation, if you are living with other individuals, is to instruct them not to touch your body under any circumstances. The suddenness of your return to your physical body when you have been free can shock the material self so it is upset for a period afterward.

If you live alone, then be sure you remind your mind as you sit down that a telephone ring will not disturb you, that a knock upon the door will not disturb you; that if either of these things happens, you will return at once without shock, with ease, to your material individuality to answer the summons. If you do not want to answer, prepare before meditating by reminding your conscious self that you will not be disturbed by any sounds.

The timing of departure and return is always perfect

if it is allowed to be so. That is, your true being will know exactly when to go forth in experience and when to return to reconnect itself with the surface being if the mind is not allowed to interfere. The best way to prepare it is by constant advice as to how it shall react to any physical activity during meditation.

There are many other things you may encounter which will be strange and new to your conscious observer, your mind, so prepare your human self ahead that whatever you meet is beautiful, wonderful, loving and one with you. If your mind is fearful it will try to interfere with your activities and it will create imaginary experiences. Your true self can be only partly free and your material self will distort unless it is educated to remaining quiet.

There is no such thing as an unhappy experience if your true being is fully free. Any unpleasantness is the action of your material mind, distorting the truth. Remember this, that you do not fear meditating again if your mind has imagined something previously.

There are no vicious individuals to attack your eternal being, for your eternal being is God, and who is there to attack God when all others of eternity are him also? There are no horrible places in which you will find your self lost, because all creation is God and so every place is him.

You will find happiness, freedom, a growing sense of exaltation beyond the physical plane, and most of all, love. Once you have passed the barriers your mind attempts to erect, you will have so many experiences you will begin living in a state of constant delight. Each experience will differ from all others. You will long to return to some because they will have been so wonderful, but always remember each one, as lovely as it was, cannot have been more wonderful than you will have. Each experience is another step forward.

You may find your self in other parts of your dimension because upon your plane there are many things to observe. You may be in some part of the earth which is across the world from you. You may find you are learning from an individual, not because he speaks to you with words but because you commune with each other in the *feeling* that is true communion.

You may find your self upon a mountain. Remember, you can step into space from that mountain and float with ease toward the ground or soar to the heavens.

You may stand before a temple and realize it is a focal point for worship where no words are spoken aloud, where you may go to remain in solitude for a time, or to be with others who are worshiping also. You will probably be delightfully surprised almost every time you meditate, once you have passed the material barriers.

Do not try to anticipate experiences which you have heard others describe, or to hope for experiences which you would like to have. You will find realization more quickly, more joyously, if you have no reservations. Freedom of thought is necessary to complete release of self, freedom *from* thought, a moving away from the processes of the human mind.

You are perfectly guided through every experience you have, so without hesitation follow that guidance. You may be spoken to by others whom you cannot see, and you may feel the words rather than hearing them. Give heed, for these are the contacts of individuals who serve,

106

whose only purpose is to give you of their strength and love that you may be helped upon your way.

You may find you are very still, not moving, perhaps not even breathing consciously with your physical body, and yet there will be nothing to fear. The functions of the material being only slow down their processes, unnecessary when *you* are not using that body for expression. So, when you go forth upon your own business, the body rests, its functions rest. Every part relaxes, gaining from your true activities the rejuvenation which causes your surface being to become fully alive to the ends of your fingertips.

If your body shows any extreme reactions to your experiences, these will only survive until you have released any fetters with which your material self attempts to hold your eternal being. Once *you* are freed your body and mind will be still.

Some time, some day, you might find your self in a place which is completely unknown to your surface being, entirely unrecognizable as a part of the planet upon which you express. This too can be accepted with calmness, because time and space, not existing beyond the material concepts of them, are not factors at all in your true being's activities. You may be upon a planet in your system, it may be a planet in another solar system, it may be a world in another dimension. Whatever it is, it will be reality, and you will enjoy every moment.

Observe about you that which is not familiar to your physical expression, that this mind may understand the world it has known does not contain even one small part as yet of what is possible to it. Take note that you feel a closeness with any individuals you meet, as if you had always known them, as if they were dear to you. You have and they are, because they are one with you. You have been drawn to them, as they have been drawn to you, for the purpose of expressing completion, for the purpose of making known to your conscious minds the allness of God.

Whether you retain a complete memory of your experiences or have no recollection at all will be totally unimportant in the effect they have on your physical expression. Of course, it is more enjoyable to your mind if it can be conscious of what you do, where you go, but it is not necessary to remember.

If you do retain contact with your surface mind, remind it that it is only an observer, a spectator. It will be inclined to make comments, to scoff, to scorn some of the truths in their simplicity and actuality.

Everything you encounter, everything you do, is not strange to your true being, but this must bring to your present consciousness the realization which your true self lives in order to impress upon your mind the constant awareness of what *you* are. This is your reason for seeking, this is your urge to seek, this is why you continue to make the effort to understand, this is the purpose in your expressing through a physical body, and this is the goal whose gaining will make it unnecessary for you to express by a material means again.

It is the purpose of your embodiment for you to understand materially what *you* are, to accept what *you* are, to express what *you* are upon the physical plane. Your mind, once accepting, will respond to the slightest direction from your true being willingly and eagerly because the human body, when it is awakened to its purpose in existing, is as easy to direct as it was difficult while unawakened. It will be as eager to serve as it was defiant in its previous ignorance. Like every part of creation, your physical body, once opened to that awareness your true self expresses, will respond every time to every part of your directing.

Enter the silence as often as you can, remembering you were not meant to relinquish your surface expression or you would not be in the material dimension. You are not meant to spend your life in contemplation or you would already have been placed in a position to do so. You might have ignored this in the past, but you would be made aware of it as you meditated. You are not meant to be or do anything except that which will bring forth complete joyousness, completion for your human self.

DEATH

Like so many things of the material world, death is only a word. Its meaning as defined in your dictionary is an ending, but in truth death, as the word is applied to the action of leaving a physical body to go forth into another plane of existence, is no ending at all.

A forward step may be termed an ending to the previous step, if you will. A move to one residence from another may be termed an ending of living in the previous abode, if you will, but these are not endings in any sense, merely changes. They are not finishes to *you*. You do not cease to exist if you step forward on your left foot, leaving your right foot in back of you momentarily. You do not cease to exist if you move from one place to another. You do not cease to exist if your form changes in size, in outline. You do not cease to exist if you complete one study and begin another, or if you finish one task and start another. You do not cease to exist if you turn a corner and walk in another direction.

You do not cease to exist, no matter what changes may take place about you. This fact has been overlooked in the worldly attitude toward death. Because an individual awareness is finished with a specific physical shell, those who do not understand have thought that individual ceased to exist, or that he had gone to some faraway location where it was impossible to reach him, where it was impossible to picture him because he would be changed in some manner beyond all recognition.

This cannot be so because it does not make sense, and every part of God is completely wise, completely explain-

110

able, completely sensible. You are changing constantly throughout your physical lifetime. From one day to another you are not expressing in exactly the same manner and from one year to the other you do not look exactly the same. As time, physical time, passes you change constantly.

This applies to every part of material living, and it applies to every part of living beyond that which you know in the present material plane. God is real, therefore everything of creation is equally real. That which you cannot see has existence fully as much as that which you can see. It is simply that it requires a shifting of focus, two different perspectives, for you to realize both are existing.

You *see* the world about you. You *hear* its sounds, but to your mind both are as real as any part of your life. You accept both equally because you are *aware* of sight and sound within your dimension. All other planes of existence are as real as the one of which you are aware at this moment. You can become aware of these planes, although they are so countless and so endless you cannot know their number or become familiar with each in this lifetime; but you can learn that they do exist, that their activities are as real and as important as yours, and that they are exactly right, fully expressing, because these are also God acting.

If you had to spend eternity within one physical body you would be confined to one type of expression, to one certain field of activity, to one certain channel of living. It is through varied expressions, varying experiences that you gain your conscious awareness of what you are, that you gain your constant understanding of what you are

111

doing, that you gain your constant being of oneness with God.

Because the pattern is simply one of living in varying forms, degrees, locations physically, it must be understood that death is only a part of a continuing flow of living, that it is only a fraction of a marvelous whole, and that it has no place in the realms of fear, of hesitation, of reluctance; all spurious emotions, products of the brain, which emanates this static and so interferes with the message the intelligence originally sent forth. The *mind* does not produce anything of itself. Understand this. It only conveys what it receives in the manner it understands.

Birth into physical life follows death from the previous dimension in which you were expressing, and death from this physical life will be a birth into the next dimension.

The action of leaving the physical body so its atomic particles may be redistributed for use elsewhere has not been understood by many individuals because their human minds have been trained to regard death with horror. They do not know what comes next and therefore they are afraid.

In God, there is complete protection. This cannot apply only to the material plane which can be seen, heard and touched by your physical being. It must apply to every part of existence. God is all there is, so God is death also, the moving forward and onward from the physical body, and trust in God produces understanding that the unknown is not a fearful thing but is so mighty in its truth it must be approached with trust and love or its might will overwhelm the human conception of what is truth.

You may have no fear of death in itself, but there are

many who do. There are many who fight the approach of the change for them. As their bodies reach a stage which informs them it will not be long before they must leave the material world they know, they become more and more terrified. They search more frantically for another "out," for a means of preserving their decaying bodies, for an acceptable belief that they can be immortal physically, for anything which will help them to forget the unchangeable fact that everything which enters the physical world will also exit from it; that everything which expresses physically is only the one thing— God, the Creator, making himself known in individual ways. If you do not have this fear you are indeed a blessed individual, blessed by your own understanding, by your own acceptance of the truth which lies within you.

Death is such a glory, such an awakening, such a great, wonderful gift that it is sometimes difficult to understand why those who have not reached awareness should have fear of it. But then there are many degrees of understanding in the physical world, and in your own understanding accept this as the reason for fear. With your own understanding reach out your heart, to love and to give of your strength to those who have no strength of their own as yet.

Let us go through the door of death, that you may see for yourself, if you have not already done so, there is nothing to fear as you approach it, as you enter it, and as you come forth upon the other side of the doorway.

First, let us forget the method of death but come to the action itself, when the eternal you has stepped forth and shed the anchor which has held it within the material world until this moment. You will suddenly feel freedom as you have not felt it in your conscious mind before. You will realize there is a beauty growing about you which makes you eager to move forward another step, that you may find what lies next, what causes such growing beauty, that you may see more and more of it. Within you has come this realization that you do not feel any fear, that you feel only lightness and freedom now that your physical body is no longer an expression of *you*.

You will perhaps feel a slight strangeness to begin with that death should be so easy, for you will remember what your conscious mind has told you for many years: Death is a horror and an end! Now that you are at the moment, now that you realize how very much mistaken the distortions of your mind were, you will turn with eagerness to that doorway and you will step through.

There is no literal doorway. There is no great divide before you. There is only the one moment when you pass from awareness of the fact that you are leaving the physical plane and are going into the consciousness that you are now within the realms of knowingness which make you completely *you*. *You* will realize you have stepped through that doorway, across that divide, with no conscious movement, with no action other than awakened realization.

What lies beyond the physical plane? There are some who teach man may not presume to know, that life and death must remain great mysteries which should not be probed by the common person; but this can only produce further ignorance, for God keeps all understanding ready for any one who wants it. You cannot be happy, you cannot do the things your Creator prompts you to do if you are not open to him. You cannot be open to him

114

unless you have that awareness which carries you into understanding, into undiluted love.

Upon the other side of the veil of death you will be more fully alive than you were in your physical being, because there will be no part of you which is asleep, which has forgotten. Every cell will be aware, for this is the next plane of consciousness and the next must always be ahead, a step forward. It must always be an upward and onward movement, and so, as you leave your physical body, you will move on to a plane of greater awareness, of greater happiness. You will have such a sense of relaxation you will not care whether you ever experience anything else again. You will be surrounded by a warmth and a love and a glow which are not only about you but within you. You are a part of all this, and it is a part of you. As you experience more and more your re-awakening to this greatness you will understand you have had this before, you have had it all through physical life. But it must remain dormant in the physical dimension until the physical being will allow it to come forth in expression.

You will have lost nothing except the drag upon your true being and you will have gained everything, for you will have become your self. All that you are you will now be able to express, and you will walk forth in confidence, fearless and free if you have prepared to accept death for what it is in truth.

There are many means of expression within the next plane, as there are upon the one you now know. You may have no need for a period of rest from the travails of your physical body. You may have no need to seek solitude for a period in order to find your balance again.

115

Your greatest desire may be to contact those for whom you have cared and who led the way for you beyond the material world.

Whatever your individual inclination may be it will be followed, for you will have no fetters upon you to hold you back, you will have no mental reservations to keep you from accomplishing whatever you are inclined to accomplish. Here too you are still individual, but the difference, the great difference, lies in the fact that you are aware of your true oneness with all things, that you will consciously be able to express your wisdom, your awareness.

You will at once see, contact your loved ones if that is your greatest desire. If your greatest need is for rest, you will rest. There is no time, so there will be no hurry in the plane beyond the physical. You will do, you will be, exactly what you are meant to do and be, and there will be plenty of time in which to do it, to be it, because this is the true eternity, without the synthetic calendar and clock systems by which you have expressed in your physical body. In complete acceptance of death, you will find not one thing you could construe as negative, as a distortion. In truth it is a great realization of eternal self.

If someone for whom you have cared has gone through this experience ahead of you, by coming to an understanding of what death really is, of what it really means, you can lose every bit of sorrow you have maintained.

Once you have learned you cannot possess anything or anybody you will be helped to understand and accept change, or death, as it is called in your world.

Once you have accepted, once you understand that

God is all things, you will no longer believe in a heaven and a hell after death. You live in heaven as a physical being if you are happy and contented. You live in hell as a physical being if you are fearful or discontented. Beyond physical life there are no such places, because God does not create punishment for one, reward for another. The laws of existence are the laws of any existence upon any plane, and your own actions automatically motivate their actions, producing experiences so you will learn and thus attain understanding.

There is no punishment beyond that which you exhibit in your physical life, beyond that which you create in your physical mind, the static which interferes with the true *you*. Any unhappiness resulting from a deed of yours is simply your means of expression, and it is a distortion of your motives in performing an action, a distortion of your understanding in regarding that action.

Once you have learned to discipline your human self, once you have learned to operate upon the physical plane by the basic law of love, you will have no need for a conception of a future life consisting of either exalted reward or horrible punishment. A God who judges would be a small God, without endless capacity, without endless power. A God who gives, after one lifetime, streets of gold and places in which to live to one individual whose life has been one of service, and then gives an eternity of fire and damnation to one whose lifetime has been a distortion of understanding, would be a monster indeed.

Reject any such conception of your God if there is even a hint of such a being in the recesses of your mind. *You* do not believe this, *you* cannot believe it because *you know. You* know you are God. *You* know God is

117

all, and *you* know God does not have one small iota of any human misconception.

As a machine frequently needs cleaning, oiling or repairing, your human body sometimes requires attention so it may cease to express, to produce things which are not true, which are not real. The machine which is producing something, if it is not running perfectly, will produce something imperfect. Your body, if it has not been cared for that it may produce perfectly, will come forth with distortion of the God-inspired motive for every action throughout your lifetime.

You, upon the other side of life, past the door of death, will understand all of this. You will understand what happened to you and why it happened, and you will prepare yourself for another expression in some manner, for existence is constant progress, constant movement, constant activity. Even in your period of resting, in that area called afterlife, you will not be at a complete standstill. Your rest will consist of complete awareness, and that is the greatest activity of all, the vital throbbing of oneness with creation itself.

Death comes in many guises to the physical plane, but its method of coming cannot mean anything beyond the reaction of the human mind to it. Just as God has made countless individuals for expression of himself, so there are countless exits by which to leave this house and go into the next. The true self does not suffer. It *cannot* suffer, for it is the Supreme Intelligence. There can be no pain inflicted upon the true being, there can be no suffering of any kind beyond that which exists in the human mind.

If someone close to you is ill and is passing because

of his illness through the veil of mystery, understand this that you do not allow an impression of suffering to affect you personally and thereby distort the love with which you regard that individual. If you will maintain a clear and true attitude, you will assist this one for whom you care so deeply in making the change. Your love undiluted will touch that one's inner being, helping it to shed the physical body without difficulty, and to move on knowing there is nothing but God, nothing but good.

If someone for whom you have cared has met a seemingly violent ending, understand that a sudden death is very often necessary because the completion of a journey has come, and in order to make way for others who are traveling the removal must be swift. The fear is only in evidence until the change comes, for the human mind contains the fear, the true mind does not.

The one who perishes by drowning, by an accident of any kind, does not feel that which it seems to feel. Since there are no accidents, since God is all love, there can be no suffering for anyone. The human body reacts according to habit, to pattern, which it has followed for all of its existence in that form.

If an individual is meeting a violent ending the body will react according to its habits, and to those who watch it will seem to be going through great suffering, great pain. But the true individual within that body does not feel it, is not conscious of it. Take this unto yourself for comfort if you must meet with a parting physically between yourself and someone else through a means you would not have chosen for that individual.

Remember that each exit is chosen by God, that he is all wise and all knowing, and so each exit must be just

119

right for each one who passes through it. Know that the feeling you have toward another individual is not for that physical expression but for the individual's self. The expression upon the material plane is simply an activity which is used by your two inner beings to express toward each other what is real and eternal. The physical bodies of themselves would not move. They would have no life in them, they would have no movement whatsoever, so you could have no feeling whatsoever. If *you*—the eternal you—were not attached to your human body and the other being was not attached to his, your material selves would have no feelings at all. Therefore, the removal of one physical body from activity can not change, it can not reduce the actual bond that is between you.

Your love is as simple to express from one dimension to another as it is when you are touching the hand of another individual with your material hand. The love you feel is as strong when it goes into the spaces beyond your human knowing as it is when you are confined with it to the planet of Earth.

How can death be an ending, when God is without end? How can death be a fearful thing, when God is all love? How can death be unknown to you, when God is available at any moment, in any place, for your investigation? How can death be anything except part of the greatness which is constant, everywhere, everything, the greatness that is God?

You must know by now that the real *you* is not the surface being who travels through his days under an earthly name. You are not John Doe, or Jane Doe. You are an everlasting being whose consciousness of self lies buried under the material mountain of your physical body and mind, until it reaches a strength beyond containing and grows in your heart until it cannot be ignored.

You are an eternal one who has in your grasp all that is necessary for you. You have the compassion to listen to others, the love to help everyone, the knowledge to move any obstacle from your pathway. You have all in your grasp that is necessary for you to survive through anything, because *you* are eternal.

This is you, this one who strives only in love and toward God. The surface shall perish when the span of earthly duties is done. It will not end in its particles, because no created material is ever destroyed, but it will re-form in some other expression which will not be you and will go on. *You,* however, will not suffer when that time is upon you, for it is not a real ending when your days upon the earth are through, but a renewal of living beyond the dimension of your present understanding.

That awareness you shall return to has been known to you before and shall be known to you more and more, until the Plan of your creation has been completed, until you return in exultation and ecstasy to the Oneness which made you to be and you shall exist for the remainder of eternity in the Oneness that is your Creator and none other.

The goal for everything in material life is material death, whether or not you are aware of it in your conscious mind. From the moment of your birth you are dying, and all of your days are but a preparation for the moment of your removal from your physical body.

In God's wisdom he made no laws which were imperfect or unwise, so do not strive to deny the facts of death. You accept seeming facts of life because they have been taught to you from your earliest time of understanding in your present physical body. Begin learning now the truth of what lies beyond this so momentary expression of *you,* that you may take your next step with eagerness.

Like awakening from sleep in a new home into which you have just moved is your passing from one dimension to another. There is no pain, there is no suffering, and so the method is not important, as has been said before.

Some individuals finish their spans in a few material years. These have had specific tasks which are accomplished within that seemingly short time. Others live what to you mortals are amazing lengths of years—eighty or ninety or a hundred. Why is this amazing, and why is it desirable? What is the urge within the human brain to cling to life after all true vitality has left the body?

It is simply that fear of what lies beyond, the old superstitious fear of death. Any time in the physical plane is but a moment. Whether you will live twenty years or two hundred years is of complete unimportance except to your individual ego, which would like to go on forever. But would God have planned with loose ends? Would he have defined a magnificent beginning for you and allowed you a miserable finish? Ask yourself in honesty and you will find only comfort in the answer.

Death is the coming of peace to the weary, of release to the sick. It is the cool breeze in summer, the warmth of dreams in the winter. It is the beginning, it is an ending, because it is change. It is the search which begins in your sphere and continues in the reaches beyond sight.

Do you not believe this because you have not been aware of existing before your physical birth? Then consider. Can you remember when you were one year old, or even what you were doing on a specific date at a specific time last year? Can you touch the sky? Can you hear the sighing of the roses? Can you see the currents of power which throb throughout your physical universe? Can you really define love? All of these are beyond your scope, and yet would you deny them? Would you say there is no God because he has not knocked upon your door in a physical form?

Many truths cannot be recognized with the physical senses. They cannot be explained satisfactorily to a completely analytical mind. They must be absorbed through the heart and thence into the brain. Open your heart to truth, and it shall be yours in your mind, surely, beyond doubt.

Know now that when your time of death is upon you it shall be a time for your rejoicing, a looking forward with high heart to the next step, and you will never fear death again. Know you shall be guided with an unfaltering hand through the narrow veil between worlds and you will not wonder how you shall take the step. Know God guards over you as the most precious of his jewels, for you *are* as precious as the most priceless.

Know there is not one thing to fear in this world or in any other. Beloved one, seek to know death and life, for you cannot find happiness if doubt makes your nights restless, you cannot find serenity if you are miserable with thoughts of what is inevitable in the future.

Yours is the heritage of all the earth and all that lies beyond if you only want it. It is to be shared by all and yet it is yours alone also. In the secret places within you where none can follow you can know the ecstasy beyond words, the awareness beyond the level of your human understanding, and you can make yours a knowing heart while it waits for that awakening beyond death. God is yours as you are his. Know this, and you shall find your true pattern, your highest contentment.

Death is the change from the material to the sublime, from one dimension to another, from one house to another. It is not an ending to anything except as you understand endings and beginnings in the material world of understanding. Death is a release from material responsibility, for recognition of self, of God.

When you learn that your loved ones are still existing, are still active in their own way, you will find comfort such as you have not found in any of your other seekings. The absence of the physical body which your material self can touch is the only thing to consider, and when you have once accomplished the realization of oneness with your loved beings in spirit you will not miss the physical absence. You must remember the physical is only an expression of spiritual self, the material expression of the eternal being, and when the spiritual self can express fully, without the barrier of the physical being, it is far beyond all material reflections of love.

Death brings a release from so many things. If you will only understand you will no longer be resentful when someone for whom you care leaves your dimension and goes into another. Remember, though, that it is not right that you should wait for death and resent life. If you can learn to live with full joy and still know that when your time comes for death you will go into that with full joy also, you will indeed be a completed being.

There are individuals upon your plane who are ready

and eager to assist you at that time when you are about to leave your physical body but have not quite stepped through into the next dimension. Your mind will not feel alone for this reason. These individuals will help you if you need help, and once you have stepped across you will find others who are ready to be of assistance also. Only the step itself is solitary, just as the step into physical birth must be. Unless your greatest urge is for solitude, you will find all of the company you need, waiting to receive you.

Death is another mile accomplished upon the road to understanding. It is the fulfillment of a promise which is held before you as a great light throughout your lifetime. If you will study nature all about you, you will see that promise in action, for each thing which seemingly dies with the seasons is reborn with a new season and is full grown, full blooming, before its time comes to die again.

The pattern is set in nature, and is obvious to any who wish to see. There is nothing hidden about it, and it is not even subtle so it would be devious to those who are slow in understanding. You will find many examples of the cycle of birth, growth and death, then rebirth if you will only look.

So the pattern runs again and again with human beings, as it does with all other parts of creation. There is beauty in each phase of existence and each new phase is more beautiful than the one before. It must be so, or God could not be as mighty as he so obviously is. As you move so must you grow, and thus it is in every part of creation.

The word "death" is just that—a *word* meaning a

change, a move from one location to another. Many, many millions have passed through the opening of death unscathed, to find the glory beyond which can be found nowhere in your material world with your material mind's seeking.

Live your life to the fullest extent. You were meant to do this, or you would not be given expression in a physical body. Extremes are distortions of the actual intent of your being, so learn to live with balance, learn to accept the truth of all there is with balance, and you will find your serenity, your acknowledgment of God which brings you to the moment of parting with a physical body without hesitation of any sort.

Go through the experience of death knowing it can only be a glorification of God. You are aware of limitations within the physical plane only because you have accepted them as real. Now become aware of the *lack* of limitations in another dimension. Accept that limitation does not apply to God in any way, and that through your active living of this knowing, through your making this your philosophy of physical life, you will be able to step into your expression of eternal life with nothing except love, complete trust in your God.

Understand for yourself, understand this truth applies to everyone and everything else so you will not sorrow over changes, so you will not resent physical removal, and above all, so you will not feel an urge to take from anything or anyone else the right to physical expression, knowing God has decided the correct time for removal.

This is the truth which lies behind the commandment, "Thou shalt not kill."

You cannot kill an individual. You can cause his material expression to cease expressing. You can stop the physical expression of an animal or of a plant, but you cannot kill the being within. Let each thing live to its full span, for its time is set by the Creator himself, and his wisdom you certainly will not question in any way when you have reached understanding of life and of death.

The two, while equal in importance, are merely two small threads in the great pattern of existence which continues unto eternity; and as you know, eternity is endless. Life is a moment's passing in the pattern of spiritual expression, death is a moment's passing in the pattern of physical expression.

Death is as real as your life now, upon the physical plane, and in the next dimension you will be as real as you are now. In the next dimension your being will express in a way which will not be the same as the present body with which you are connected. Understand this. Everything of your existence has reality when it is a true, undiluted expression of self, God. It does not matter which plane contains your expression. Each is a material dimension in the sense that it is real to you while you are expressing in that dimension.

You have perhaps always considered that only the physical has reality, when the truth is that all reality is eternal, and the temporary things with which you feel you must cope are distorted reflections of reality, having no separate reality of their own.

Yes, life is real because it is one plane of expression through which God is being active. Yes, death is real because it is another plane of expression through which God is being himself. One has no more reality than the

other and no less reality .The difference lies in the awareness you express of the beauty which every plane contains.

Death can only be beautiful, right, perfect, because it
too is a part of the Divine Pattern. You are a part of the
Divine Pattern also. It is your destiny to meet the death
which comes to all physical expressions, and it is the intent of your pattern to take that step in full confidence
and in full awareness this is God walking through his
own creation.

May you assimilate this quickly, that you will never
again have fear, that you will never again wonder what
will happen next because you are afraid that without
knowing exactly what it is, it *must* be something horrible.

May you gain acceptance and understanding of the
activities of those who are no longer with you materially.
May you find in this understanding all you need to overcome any unhappiness you have known in regard to
death, all you need to bring you peace, joyous expectancy,
complete contentment, now and forevermore.

REINCARNATION

Every human being is a testimonial to God's greatness. Each part of the earth and of the invisible skies is further proof of his awesome power and wisdom.

How then can God be fitted into a human category of behavior, a human conception of his pattern of action? Obviously, God is far more than human. Obviously, he is far more than anything of the physical plane.

If your Creator made one being with every desirable attribute and another with none, he could not be balanced in his own Being. If your Creator gave you only one opportunity to earn the right to eternity in heaven after death, he would be far less than any understanding parent of the mortal plane. If your Creator punished you forever for making an error (reflecting truth with distortion) in ignorance, he would be less knowing than a prison board of human beings who parole a convict that he may have a "second chance" to do things the right way.

How much happier is the picture of a God who loves all things boundlessly, equally, who always gives a fresh opportunity to any who have lost the way, who always offers his comfort and protection to any who are afraid!

One lifetime, important or obscure, can hardly prove God's impartiality or deny his love. No matter what kind of God you believe in, surely it is a strong, all-powerful Being who gives you a real faith.

Confining the Creator to a human behavior pattern in the limited minds of men has set the course of the present world turmoil and all past world turbulences.

God is pictured as a human-like Being who favors one country over another, one religion over another, one individual over another. God has been confined for thousands of years to the human-conceived behavior of punishing endlessly with torture "mistakes"—even one "mistake"—made in the span of a few physical years; of rewarding eternally with a vague, heaven-state the "virtues" clung to over a short physical lifetime.

If this was truth, there would be no one at all in heaven and hell would have become so overcrowded long ago there would be no room for any more transgressors!

No mortal who has ever trod the earth has passed through his lifetime without any mistakes, not even the great ones. This is a flat statement, which makes it a dangerous one, for flat statements leave themselves open to being disproved. However, these words are written with full awareness of their controversial nature. Anything which challenges precedent, habit, custom, is upsetting to the average point of view, usually so unawakened.

You who seek your own truth must become accustomed to finding things which are opposite to or far deviating from the pattern for civilized behavior, the rules for civilized acceptance. In your broadening awareness that things, in truth, are not always or even seldom what they seem to be on the surface, you can accept certain facts which might have upset you in the past.

Look now, in your opening consciousness, at the statement that there is no one individual who has lived a life of physical perfection throughout his span. There are some individuals who *seem* to have been expressing purest virtue, self-sacrifice, constant good, who were not "human" in action or in thought. But even the great ones were not this "divine" materially. Until they *realized,* became aware of and *accepted* what they were, they distorted truth to some extent.

The human mind will transmit truth at all times, but that truth will not be pure and completely undiluted until the entire being is freed to express on the physical plane. Jesus made "mistakes," Buddha committed "errors," Lao-Tze did not always understand, Krishna "criticized" his enemies. All expressed some human distortion, until they came to their individual moments of enlightenment, when they ceased to be human beings in consciousness and became divine selves *using* their mortal forms for expression.

Look at your own life for an example of this truth. What you seem to be to the rest of your world is only a part of what you are in your surface person, and what you are in your surface person is only a part of what you are aware of being beneath that surface.

You, like everyone else who has ever lived on a mortal plane, have undoubtedly performed deeds or at least have had thoughts you would not wish others to discover. You have no doubt kept very secret at least one deed, at least one mental action, you have felt was shameful, dishonest, or a big mistake in some way.

You are like all other human beings in this respect. No expression of God in physical form is pure "virtue," pure behavior in every way until he becomes so powerful in his conscious awareness of self his understanding goes far beyond the present awareness of his planet.

When that light breaks within the mind, the time for activity in the material dimension becomes very short.

Read the histories of your great religious leaders, of your saints and heroes. Their spans, once they began performing noble deeds, doing wonderful works, were extremely limited. They were removed from your plane suddenly and swiftly when their patterns were completed.

Probe the history of any of these outstanding ones and you will find a human being. You will find a man or a woman who had thought and acted much as you may have in the past, without a very individual motive or attitude. You will find, after all, the only difference between this great one and you is that his or her unique, outstanding quality making the greatness was not the unique, outstanding quality making yours. Each one has an individual quality, none greater or less great. It is *awakening* to realization that brings forth this quality, in any figure of history, in you.

Therefore, there cannot be any "better" or "worse" people. There cannot be "wicked" people, so there is no need for a hell to which they may be confined after they leave their physical shells. This would mean God was confining parts of his own Being to eternal torment, a completely senseless act.

There cannot be "virtuous" people, so there is no need for a heaven where harps are strummed forever and the favored few sit around on clouds throughout eternity. This would mean God was confining parts of his own Being to endless musical effort, endless sitting, a silly act indeed.

God, being boundless, without limitation, cannot be confined anywhere. All of creation, being God, cannot be bound anywhere for any reason. Only the unawakened consciousness is limited or confined. This it does to itself.

God cannot be both bad and good as the material mind understands the definitions of these words. He is everything, so the "bad" and the "good" are manifestations of him, *but they are the same, not* opposing qualities. He is all that *seems* to be "bad," or "wicked," but the lack of understanding does not makes this "badness" a fact. It is an imaginary quality, a distorted truth, as are any unhappy, upsetting parts of your world.

You must learn to "stand upon your own two feet," to walk without the crutches of anyone's opinions, if you would reach understanding, acceptance, awareness. You cannot take for your own the pronouncements of anyone else, be he churchman, heretic, king — or writer! You can only find the truth that will bring you happiness within your own being. You *can* belong to a religious organization and be completely contented in the teachings of that religion *if* it offers the truths to which your being responds through the individual you. You *can* follow a teacher or leader and be completely contented with listening to his lessons *if* his teachings offer the truths already within.

You will find intelligent individuals who are completely opposite in their viewpoints on any subject in your world. You will find honorable individuals on both sides of any controversy. You will find wonderful individuals whose religions are contradictory. While this may have confused you in the past, there is no need for it to confuse you any longer.

In the physical dimension, God obviously does not express himself in one way only. If he did, there would not be animal, plant and mineral kingdoms but just *one* expression, all parts of that one identical and all going through the same physical actions.

Humanity is one branch of God, and each man is a separate twig which still belongs to the whole tree. Two individuals can see a matter from two opposing sides, from two sides of the tree, because everything does have more than one side, one approach. This explains why both can be right when they have opposing viewpoints. They are standing with their backs to each other, looking toward the outer edges of the matter. Once both turn and look toward the center, they find invariably that there *is* a meeting-point, a place of balance, where they come to a complete agreement.

Any argument or difference in your world can be resolved if it is turned from argument to discussion, from resentment to understanding, from a focus on controversial points to a focus on the balancing area. There are no quarrels except the imaginary differences of the human dimension, to which surface beings persist in clinging because they do not understand how to look beyond that which is directly before their eyes, because they are afraid they will be lost if they let go of personal insistence.

There are no quarrels if individuals are happy. There are no belligerently insistent opinions expressed if individuals are self-accepting, assured of equal importance in life's pattern.

The greatest dissensions today are not because of the subjects under question but because of the dissenters. The biggest point of argument between religious denominations is not their teachings but their influential positions, not their truths but their membership ambitions.

Church dignitaries are as human as anyone else, and are therefore prone to introducing their personal convictions into the religions they teach. This is not derogatory, not criticism. These individuals too are expressing as they know how to express, are being what their awarenesses of self are free to be. If their understanding is not limitless, who can say they are wrong?

Whatever your religion may be, there is no quarrel with it. The one important thing to remember is that anything which makes you happy is *right* for you.

Religion, churches, centers, organizations, are fine, as long as they do not insist individually that they are the only way to God, that theirs is the only right way in which to spend Sundays or Saturdays or any specific day of the week sacred to them.

Unorganized religion, individual faith is fine, as long as the individual expressing it does not insist all churchgoers, members of groups, are blind fools worshipping false idols.

These words are fine, as long as they do not jar against your truly firm convictions, clash with your deepest acceptance of God. If they do, it is best you turn to another section,-or put this book down and forget it.

If you are still seeking, are open-minded about creation, God, your own being, give your attention and wait until you understand the meanings of what you hear or read from others. The only way you will ever find the answers to your own questions is to open the door to your inner being, who can and will supply you with the knowledge you seek. The answers from others are stop-gaps until you have found your own.

Your acceptance or rejection of the question of reincarnation, rebirth, may have been based in the past upon what you have heard from others—the opinions of those who seemed important to you for some reason. Have you actually given this matter your personal attention, your personal consideration? It is far more vital to your happiness, your serenity, than you may have realized.

Rebirth cannot be written off as a subject not worth mentioning by those who are seeking truth with sincerity. There is no question regarding life, physical or otherwise, which can be ignored except by the unknowing.

Reincarnation has been judged and found wanting by many who profess to know all of the answers about God and his ways. It has been criticized, reviled, ridiculed, then ignored by such as these, but they have offered no alternative suggestions as to where individualized creation was before and where it will be after material expression.

Reincarnation can no longer be relegated to the category of unimportant side issues in the continuing material struggle between opposing factions. It cannot be treated any longer as a figment of deluded imaginations because there are too many intelligent individuals who accept it.

The questions of why you are here, where did you come from, where are you going, are hardly unimportant, nor are they to be considered mysteries beyond your understanding, answers you have no right to seek. You cannot escape facing these questions some time during your physical existence. As a unit of God, the Creator, you have the right to seek and find your answers.

There is no unfathomable mystery in the pattern of living. You have been surrounded by obvious examples from your first moments of consciousness in your present dimension. A plant flowers during the growing season. The flowers wilt and die, and the plant seems to die also, but when the season for growing things appears again, up comes the plant, fresh, rejuvenated, to produce its blooms once more. The eternal self of that plant does not die. Its physical expression completes a purpose, then is disposed of for other purposes. The newest expression is materially fresh, but the same eternal self activates it.

A tree produces fruit which ripens and dies. The tree's leaves fall, it lies quiescent until the freshening season comes again. Then it produces leaves, blossoms, fruit, as if death had not touched its branches.

The hairs upon your head grow, fall out and are replaced by other hairs. Your nails grow, are trimmed so the farthest ends are finished, but the root ends continue to push forward.

Your entire body is a collection of cells, living and dying, being replaced. This process is constant, as long as your physical being expresses. When the time comes for *you* to leave your material vehicle, the atoms which comprise your surface structure will be put to other uses, changed in formation but not in their basic forms.

You, as all parts of the eternal God, are indestructible. All of the words of all who would deny it cannot change this truth. They cannot change the fact that *you never die.* This is the immortality referred to in the Bible. Whether you express on your present plane or in some other dimension, *you* are real, *you* are active, *you* are your self. Your mode of expression changes constantly, every moment, but *you* do not change from what you are, have always been, will always be.

Fear-peddlers, hate-mongers, would convince you of

their own fears and hatreds, their own lack of understanding, for they are imprisoned by their distortions. Believe with all your heart that no one with a full, loving trust in God would insist on your believing in anything, let alone in a Creator who is less than perfect. No one with a happy trust in God's Plan would insist there is anything to fear, past, present or future. A balanced individual will not teach fear to others, for he has no fears himself. An unbalanced individual is unawakened and hardly qualified to point the way for others to walk.

Whether you accept reincarnation or not is entirely your privilege. Make it yours, though, and not someone's insistence or prompting. If you can see *for yourself*, with happiness and faith for future physical events, that *you* express continuously until the eventual rejoining, then you have accepted reincarnation, rebirth, as fact.

The light of understanding cast on any darkness brings love, trust. Once understood, any human inclination to fear is dissolved instantly, for it is shown in the light as being without any substance.

Without a clear perspective, the law of rebirth might seem to the unknowing as great a threat as the "hell" of conventional religion. Most of all, the unknowing would fear it because it places the responsibility for all of physical life's pattern squarely on each individual. Unfortunately, many human beings were long ago trained to and therefore have formed the habit of rejecting personal responsibility for anything.

When understood, reincarnation becomes the great love with which God plans physical expression. Because mistakes are simply distortions of truth, they are made only by the unaware. Far from being marked for "punishment," they are marked for *balancing,* which will awaken understanding.

Is this not wisdom? Is this not an example of God's all-knowingness? It is human misconception, unawakened awareness, which causes the lack of recognition, understanding of his laws. In the material world, an individual who makes a mistake and is "caught" is punished by his fellow beings. Those who make similar "mistakes" usually do not allow him to forget that they know of his "transgression."

This is material thinking, material attitude. Because it is so limited in comparison to God-understanding, it is vitally necessary for you to understand that *thinking* is human, bound, and *understanding* is pure God, boundless. It is necessary, if you would reach knowing, that you train your mind to acceptance of the fact that Creation is far more than the material world, so Truth is far more than the small parts of it understood by the material world in general. Remember, lack of understanding cannot lessen truth, cannot make it other than what it is. Lack of understanding covers truth with a mask, covers it with a veil, distorts the clear vision of it.

Keep this in your mind as you study life. Facts cannot be changed, but they can and certainly are covered over, misunderstood. Remind yourself constantly that surface appearances are not always to be accepted for what they seem to be. You will become more understanding, happier with your own circumstances, if you do this.

You were born into your present dimension to express God in your individual surface way, for his purposes, not your material determinations. When your assignment, whatever it may be, has been completed, *you* will leave

139

this plane and express in another. *You,* your eternal consciousness, will *not* cease to exist, you will *not* stop expressing, you will *not* lose awareness. The misunderstanding of this truth is due to the misconception that the physical mind is the center, the producer, the motivating power of the material being. This, of course, cannot be. If it were correct, you could not sleep because you would be dead once your mind lost consciousness. You could not survive an anaesthetic or a faint.

After physical "death," *you* will be as active as, perhaps more active than, you have been throughout your "life." Eventually, you will again be ready for expression through another vehicle, still following God's purposes. You may incarnate (express) in another dimension, in another world. Whatever you do, wherever you go, you will still always be the Supreme Intelligence of God in action.

Only the physical mind, the machine, which is not being controlled by the true self, could fear or reject such a beautiful fact. Only the self-imposed limitations of the human brain could produce doubt regarding God's ability, his wisdom.

What *are* some of the fears of the unawakened regarding reincarnation? Are they guilty apprehension? Are they hesitations about any unknown destination? Are they focused on a dread that loved ones will be gone, forever lost by the gulf, the separation of rebirth?

First, remember God does not judge or punish. Your actions, your motives, your attitudes are in your own hands and likewise, your lessons, your balancing, your growth are within the jurisdiction of your eternal self. Remember there is no slightest deviation from total, all-encompassing love beyond the planes of unawakened understanding.

Second, remember God is present everywhere at all times. You cannot go in any direction that he is not taking each step you take, turning each corner you turn. There is not one fearsome goal in existence, so your destination must always be a wonderful one.

Third, remember God's wisdom covers every facet of existence, in *all* dimensions. His own being is the love you feel within, no matter how you express it. This love could hardly be confined to one lifetime and then forgotten by That which love is. The pattern of reincarnation, therefore, is cut so certain individuals work out their destinies together. Although you meet and learn to know all parts of God's expressions eventually, by certain groups do the Creator's individualized selves, do you, move toward eternal oneness. Those who have been close will be close again and those who have been enemies will finally come to friendship and love.

There are no casual encounters in your life, no accidental meetings. Every person, every event, every experience is a lesson of some kind in your school of creation. You are not conscious, of course, of what each thing offers at the time of its offering, but the impression is made upon you nevertheless, and its result will be of use to you at some time.

How such intricate actions can be made to move so smoothly, so perfectly, is not to be pondered. Such wisdom is beyond containing in your material mind but can, by opening to inner knowing, make your surface self aware.

Everyone, everything follows the pattern of rebirth.

Entry from any dimension into another is birth, or more correctly, rebirth. An awakening while you are on the physical plane is a rebirth—a rebirth to that awareness with which you are fully endowed, of which you are seldom conscious.

Real love does not die, as *you* do not die, so never fear a continuing life because you have thought you could only rejoin your loved ones in heaven. Real love does not change, it does not stop. When there is true love between individuals, it lasts from one lifetime to another and beyond, throughout eternity.

Thousands of years can have passed since a loving experience between two beings. Still they will recognize each other when their paths cross again. It may be they will not be conscious of the reason for the attraction. It may manifest itself as the attraction between friends, it may manifest itself as the attraction between a man and a woman, or it may manifest itself as impersonal admiration. But there will be a pull between two beings who have ever loved truly, since the feeling cannot be erased or changed.

Sometimes the recognition between members of the opposite sex is misunderstood, and where there has been great love in the past between brother and sister, mother and son, father and daughter, or between two friends, due to the habit patterns of the surface mind it may be defined in the present as the physical attraction between a man and a woman, and the individuals will act accordingly. They will bring forth experiences with unpleasant conclusions because they have not understood the attraction. Many unhappy marriages can be traced to this cause.

Here is another important reason for understanding reincarnation, for understanding self. There can be a closeness without any desire or need for surface closeness. There is a spiritual oneness with all things, but the *consciousness* of that spiritual oneness must be felt if it is not going to be distorted into an action which was not meant to take place, thereby creating a karmic condition which must be balanced and is one more boulder upon the path of progress toward completion.

An instant dislike, resentment or hatred between two individuals who have not met before in the present lifetime and have no known reason for their reactions can be explained by reincarnation. At some period in the past one or both of these beings have performed an activity which was ignorant upon the other. They may have been on opposing sides in a war, one may have been cruel to the other, one may have caused great unhappiness, disaster or pain to the other. But you can be sure there was distortion between the two, and the memory of this persists until it is balanced between them in a right way.

Any distorted action upon the part of one individual toward another will be balanced. All of these things cannot be done in one lifetime. Again, a point for reincarnation. A ruler of the past who did not use discretion in his or her actions but was motivated by selfish reasons may have affected the lives of thousands of individuals. This person must balance with every one of those individuals before he or she can get past the huge blockade in the path. If there are five hundred thousand people whose lives were affected by the actions of this ruler, that one will balance with five hundred thousand deeds before being finished with that experience. Sometimes many thousands of years pass before the balancing is completed, but it will be finished and not one individual will be left from that balancing.

The sooner you open your physical being to eternal truth, the less material experiences will be necessary to balance your pattern. As you begin to understand, you will recognize your experiences for the lessons they contain, accept them for the forward movements they make. Then, when your awareness reaches a constant stage, when you can look upon all of life from the calm center of your true being, the material lessons will be needed no longer.

Letting truth flow through you from within is like opening a gate to the floodwaters of all good things. The only effort involved is the setting-aside of any barriers, painfully erected by mortal ignorance. If you can instantly control your surface self, no effort of any kind is needed.

The truth of reincarnation is not intended to cause you to step carefully in fear lest you should do something which you will have to balance with unpleasantness in the future. It is far better to do something and require a balancing than it is to stand still and do nothing, for then you will be forced into a step eventually. The prompting, the urging of the inner being can be denied only for a time. Then it can no longer be ignored, and you will find yourself making a sudden move without intention, an incorrect move. It is better to do what you think might be right, for then a distortion is at least an honest attempt within the limits of your understanding.

Reincarnation is a beautiful truth, for it offers hope

to everyone who has piled so-called mistake upon mistake in the present lifetime, it offers a great destiny to everyone who believes he has found only failure in the present lifetime, it offers unfoldment to everyone who has not found his own God in this lifetime. It offers a security, it gives a material future, it holds promise of glories beyond description. It is like the flower which unfolds to the sunlight. The wider the petals spread, the more parts the sun can reach and the deeper it can penetrate. With each lifetime you unfold a little more to the light of God. It penetrates your surface being from within a little more strongly, and each time warms you more constantly with its power.

It is the surface personality alone who ceases to function in its present form when the time has come for you to have reached the balance of your days. It is your surface being alone who can be discouraged when everything seems to be going in the wrong direction. It can only be your surface person who refuses to accept the truth, it can only be your surface person who is unhappy, unfulfilled, unknowing.

You are all of these things; and when you are not expressing through a physical body you will realize you contain them all. You will see your past incarnations, you will understand what took place in your most previous incarnation, what needs to be balanced in your surface consciousness-to-be, and you will prepare your self for the next physical expression.

In your true being, in the spaces of eternity, you will find ecstasy beyond your dreams. You cannot imagine it because it is beyond the human quality of imagination. You will behold the light of God to an extent such as your human self could not face, for it is brighter than the sun, more powerful than the lightning, greater than the universe.

You have been held prisoner of a mass misconception of God and of all his Creation, unless you are a free, happy, loving individual. To release yourself from this prison, all that is necessary is to let your inner being give you the true picture of existence, and to close your mental door to the persistent knocking of material ignorance.

If you can accept that this is but one of many lifetimes, that you have lived before and will live again on a physical plane, you will understand why there is no cause for fear of any kind at any time. You will not be injured by an accident, for there are no accidents. You will only be injured if you have injured another, and this you can learn to accept as the balancing of a deed which can then be forgotten in the understanding you do harm to yourself when you harm another, because everyone, every thing is you.

You will not die until your time comes to die, and then it cannot be prevented, its method cannot be set aside. But no matter what human dangers you face before that time comes, no matter how ill your body apparently is, no matter how deadly a peril seems to be, you are physically safe until the time of *your* departure is come. When that time does come, *you* will go with ease from your material body into the spaces, consciously, at once and without fear, if you have prepared your mind by complete understanding of this fact.

Open yourself to the joy of knowing there is no such thing as only one chance for anybody. Open yourself to

146

the happiness of knowing God is your guide in every dimension.

Open yourself without reservation to all that is beyond the confines of the finite world, open that you will no longer fear living or dying. They are both a part of the same thing.

You have lived before in a physical body, you will live again in a physical body. More than that, *you live* wherever you are, *you* go on forever!

LOVE

The greatest need of the human self is for love. You can have all the wealth your coffers will hold, all the fame your world can offer, all the education your schools can teach. You can have had your every other wish fulfilled, your every other dream come true, but if love is not among these you will be empty, barren. The need to express love is so vital your physical body is affected if you have no way of giving of your deepest self.

How can mere words express the truth about love? It is the most overwhelming thing in existence. It is the basis of all activity. It is the cause of all creation and it is the goal of all seeking.

Love cannot be confined to words, it cannot be confined within any boundaries regardless of all effort by the human mind to imprison it. Love, undistorted, undiluted, is so powerful it cannot be detoured, it cannot be detained, it cannot be ignored, it cannot be conquered.

As love expresses it grows, and as it grows it expands in all directions so there is no limit to where it goes, to whom or what it touches, to how it expresses itself.

The human conception of love has, for the most part, been based upon the attitude that love is a physical expression between individuals—between man and woman, between parent and child, between brother and sister, between friends. But these are merely small examples of that which lies within you and everything of creation striving to free itself to express in consciousness the God which love is.

Love is a blending of all that exists. It is the beauty

before your eyes, it is the music within your ears, it is the softness beneath your fingertips. It is the knowing in closeness of others. It is the realization of God in moments when you are alone and can feel the silence which exalts you above your physical being.

The word "love," expressed aloud, is reacted to by every individual who hears it with some thought, some picture, in each individual mind, which is connected with that word. Even the unhappiest of individuals respond to the word "love," perhaps with a memory, perhaps with a lift of the heart, perhaps with a longing which grows in strength at each mention of the word.

If you would understand love for yourself, if you would realize the great need of its expression in your life, if you would know why it is absolutely essential to your being that love is an activity within you and around you, absorb this truth.

Let us return to the basic fact before all other facts. There was God and nothing else before the material worlds were created. God, a force, a power, whatever you would call him, was complete and entire within himself, or itself. Because this self was love everything God caused to express individually in the material channel was composed solely of love. There was nothing else and there is nothing else.

The power which carries you beyond the doorway of the material plane is love. The power which overcomes any situation, any individual who has enmity toward you, any distance or any time, is love. The meditation in which you seek your own God is motivated by love. The deeds you perform to help others upon your physical plane are caused by love.

149

Everything you do, every desire you express, every longing you feel, is caused by love, for your basic being, the eternal you, is love, love, love. There *is* nothing else, there *can be* nothing else, for God is nothing else, and all is God.

You cannot stifle love and be happy, healthy, completely alive. The suppression of love is a slow strangling of the most vital element in your nature and it kills as effectively as a knife. You might live to the age of ninety without love, but you would have been dead to all intents and purposes long before. This is not the death which comes when you change dimensions, the glorious step, but is the dreary "nothing" state of the human conception of a vacuum. Only love in some form can keep you completely alive and enchanted with life.

If you will add the two plus two of the facts of creation, you will find the inevitable four of the answer that since one material is available with which to make something, whatever the product may be, the material of that product continues to be what it was originally. Therefore, you were created from love, you express as love, and you will continue to exist forever as love.

Love can be distorted by the habit patterns of the human mind until the mind has persuaded itself that love is hate, but this is not true.

Many times it has been said that hate is akin to love, and these words are truth because hate is love distorted. You cannot hate. It is literally impossible to hate, because in your basic self where only love exists there can be no expression of anything except love, and when it comes forth upon the surface and you give it the name of hate, you are only deluding yourself about an emotion which does not exist.

There is no such thing as hate. There cannot be. When you react extremely to another individual, you should seek the causes beyond the surface, because what seems to be upon the surface cannot be the truth if your emotion is one of hatred. It is an imitation emotion, a synthetic expression which has no existence whatsoever except as you imagine it to exist.

When you react with resentment to what another has said or has done, apparently, to you, you are not really reacting with resentment but you are reacting from a motive of love. If you will seek beyond your seeming resentment and find understanding of the other individual's motives, you will find you have erased the supposed resentment and understanding has taken its place. What is understanding except love?

If you are afraid at any time, you are simply unknowing of the truth that there is nothing to fear, there can be nothing to fear, because all things are love. Seek beyond that fear, seek to understand what it is you think you are afraid of, and why you think you are afraid, and you will come—again—to understanding that you have passed beyond the fear, which never even existed, and you are reacting with love to that which you believed you had feared.

If you would inflict cruelty upon another individual, upon an animal, upon any part of God's creation, pause first. Seek the reason why you wish to express toward that person or that thing and you will find beneath your supposed reason the true one, which was an urge to act with love.

151

All of this may seem to you at first only so many words. Through the habit patterns of your world, throughout your lifetime, you have been accustomed to reacting to various situations and individuals with varying degrees of emotion, not reason. You have been accustomed to resenting seeming injustices performed upon your person. You have been accustomed to disliking or hating others who seem to infringe themselves upon your rights as a human being. You have been accustomed to fearful, worrisome thoughts about situations whose endings you could not see or whose solutions seemed impossible to overcome.

All you need to do is to change your habit pattern of thinking, to train your mind to open itself to the true pattern which is expression upon the surface of the feeling self within, to erase the imaginary emotions with which you have attempted to live and have found you cannot do so with happiness, with serenity, because they are not—they are *not*—balanced emotions, they are not real expressions.

Only love can make you happy and serene. Only by understanding what love is, only by understanding it is all there is, only by learning to express this allness can you find what you seek. It is already yours; you have only to claim it.

The basis of everything, remember, is love. When you seek meditation, to relax yourself, your body and mind, you will approach it with a love for your eternal being, with a love for the God which you are and which causes you to express individually. You will speedily find that relaxation and that awareness which have been described before.

When you seek to develop any ability, if you will approach your seeking with love, you will develop your ability much more rapidly than if you seek only with an eagerness to learn. Although this eagerness itself is love, you must be conscious of the fact to use it to its fullest degree of power.

In telepathic development, when you understand it is simple because you are one with the individual you are seeking contact with, you will be in contact the instant your understanding comes to you.

When you seek to understand death, when you seek to understand the reality of your loved ones who are not with you on the material plane, the love which is understanding will so fill you as you accept it you will never again give thought to the physical absence of those you have known, or to the invisibility of the true existence beyond the plane you know.

You will understand this is only one of many expressions, that others are as real as yours. You will be filled with love so there is no room for fear of things you do not know as yet. There will be no room for trepidation when you consider your step through the doorway between this plane and the next one.

When you seek to understand anything with the proper attitude, you will be filled with love the moment that understanding is accepted by you. Understanding *is* love. This has been said before. But how many times can it be said and still be said again? You cannot say too often what is true, because the words are so inadequate they *must* be repeated again and again if they are to be impressed upon the mind, until it can open to the *feeling* from within which contains the truth without words.

153

Do you know what love really is? Do you understand that love is God and God is all? Do you understand that in those words you are reading the whole truth and that you need no other? If God is all there is, and love is all of God, then you need only to accept and express love to touch upon all of wisdom, to realize all of realization, to express all there is to express.

Consciousness of love must enter your mind, or all of the words of all of the books in the world will be empty to you. Train your mind now to accept that the definition of love with which you have lived in your lifetime as a physical being is inadequate and incomplete.

Love is not the taking by an individual from another individual. Love is the giving of self without thought for how much is given, for what rewards will be returned. In the joy of giving love there is no room for anything else but a complete concentration upon that which you are giving. You will have no concern for what others think of you, you will have no concern for what others do to you, you will have no concern for what others give to you, when you are expressing love in its purest form, in its true motive.

When you give to one who is in material need, if you feel a deep joy and an humble gratitude that you are privileged to share with another, you are expressing love.

When you care for a child, and you care for that child with the deepest feeling of gratitude that you are so honored to have within your responsibility the care of a human life, you are expressing love in its purest form, and you will be one of those who does not *demand* obedience, who does not *demand* anything of the child. You will be too full of the expression of your feeling, you will be too full of your own desire to give to that child for any demand or even any wish for a return. You will not hope the child will show its gratitude as it gets older by giving you attention and by caring for you materially, for when your task is finished and the child has become an adult, you will let it go freely, grateful that you have accomplished your task successfully, and again you will give humble thanks that it was your great privilege to care for this human being until he was ready to care for himself.

If you have a task to perform and you are wholeheartedly engrossed in that task with the attitude that you want to give it your best, that it is very important in the scheme of God's creation, that it is a task which was given to you to do, you will not be concerned with what it may be, you will not be concerned with rewards you may get, because in love expression the true reward is in the moment of actual giving, of actual doing. The material rewards which might come after are very small indeed when measured against the inner feeling of giving.

When you are with a friend and you can express toward that friend your complete acceptance of him as he is, you are giving love in its purest form. A friend does not criticize another for being or doing anything. A friend accepts another exactly as he is, and understands his seeming faults and less pleasant habits are only individual expressions of his being, and that these surface things have absolutely nothing to do with the bond which makes real friends so close. In being a friend, you have your own reward. You do not demand another be a friend to you if you are truly a friend.

In closeness with another individual, the closeness beyond all others, you have the opportunity to give such as will not come to you as fully under any other circumstances, because this is the opportunity, this is the situation in which the creation God caused to exist becomes whole again.

Do not be afraid of the fact that there are two of everything in existence. There is male and there is female, and in God's wisdom there is cause for this. How can God have made any mistakes? How can anything of his creation be less than anything else? How can it have something wrong with it, how can it be anything which is shameful or hateful, or to be misunderstood? For completion, there must be two. Upon the surface there must be two of anything. Living creatures reproduce their like when a male and a female become one. Living plants reproduce when a male and a female plant have become one, through the services of the winds, the birds and the insects.

When in time your scientists' studies have disclosed the fact that there are male and female rocks, that there are male and female grains of sand, you will understand this more fully, if you wish to wait until this disclosure is made.

If you do not wish to wait, if you do not need to have physical, surface proof presented to you by those whose studies you think qualify them to know better than you, then accept the truth now. There is no wisdom you cannot have, because it is all about you, everywhere, and it is free to anyone who cares to tap the source. Within you is that source.

Within you is *all* truth, *all* knowledge, *all* understanding, *all* awareness; and when you open yourself to it you will find it there, as it has always been there.

156

Understand love, and you have conquered the world. Express love, and you have reached the pinnacle, the highest pinnacle, any human being can reach. Know love, and you have absorbed all wisdom to you, to any part of eternity.

The rest of wisdom, of understanding, are simply minor branches of the one great fact. To know how to meditate is to express love. To learn to communicate telepathically is to express love. To live in peace and harmony with your world is to express love. To accomplish your daily tasks successfully is to express love.

You can do nothing, you can be nothing, you can see nothing, you can hear nothing, you can touch nothing, you can become nothing that is not love. Love is endless, love is forever. It touches everything there is. It *is* everything that exists, Love *is* all. The sooner you accept that, understand it, make use of it, the sooner you will be finished with any seeming misery you are clinging to today.

You are love. You are a wonderful person because you are love, and no matter how you have expressed in the past, what surface expressions you have made, you are expressing love, and the only reason it seems to have been anything else is because you did not understand this fact.

If you are alone among mortals, it is only because you did not understand, because you did not understand love. You are never alone within your being, and there is no need for anything else. When you can accept the love within you in its all-encompassing truth, you will lose your feelings for anything else.

When you can spend each day in constant awareness that God is expressing through you and therefore love is expressing through you, you will draw to you all of your supply, all of the individuals who are to come within your orbit, all of the experiences you need to pass through in your lifetime to walk another step on the path of enlightenment.

Consciousness of love draws it to you as a magnet draws to itself. Consciousness of love makes others aware of you, because the love within them recognizes yours and pulls the surface beings in your direction. Consciousness of love makes you a success materially, in whatever field you are meant to succeed. All are not intended to become famous in this lifetime, all are not intended to become hugely wealthy in this lifetime, all are not intended to explore the material world in this lifetime as a task to perform, a lesson to learn, a goal to accomplish.

Your goal, accomplished, will make you fully as ecstatically happy as the accomplished goal of the greatest king, of the richest tycoon, of the most intrepid explorer in this world of yours. You, individually, when you have accomplished the task which was set by your own being before you began to express in your present physical body, will give yourself completion and fulfillment beyond any question of doubt, and this action is love in some form of expression.

You will operate upon this one great, basic, eternal truth, whether you are aware of it or not. If you are not aware of it your human self is miserable because it is squirming beneath the pressure of the desire to know the truth and to express the truth. Once you have gained the consciousness of truth and have trained your human self to express it, you will no longer have that pressure upon you. It will remove itself at once.

Remember, all *emotion* comes from the one *feeling* of love. All emotion stems from this one plant and flowers according to the individual understanding of that truth.

Love cannot be confined to a room, a house, a city, or a world. It cannot be confined in an individual, it cannot be confined in any one thing. It *is* all things, it is a part of all things, it is the entirety of all things, and it is the joining force of all things.

Love is not simply an emotion. It is *the* creation. It is the feeling within you of awareness, of ecstatic oneness with God. It is the knowledge that you are so much more than you have suspected in the past.

Love is all that you are, and when you can know this beyond doubt watch the repercussions in your material world. Watch the adjustments in your daily activities, watch the response from others. These things will seem like miracles to you, for miracles are simply actions resulting from a concentrated application of the awareness of love.

The channel of power, the magnetic current, is love permeating your earth's atmosphere, constantly making itself known to you through your body if you will give it your attention.

Love is impersonal, and yet it is the most personal thing you can know. Love is so expansive it is endless, and yet it is contained in the tiniest insect upon your planet. Love is all things, and it is the one thing most important to you.

Love is a giving, love is a sharing. And beyond that, far beyond that, it is awareness, for awareness, once accomplished, does not require a physical action. It does not require that you hold out your hand with a gift in it, or that you open your mouth and emit words of kindness, for awareness is the state of *being*, the state of being is the activity of expressing God, and the activity of expressing God is simply *knowing* love is you, you are love.

In the human mind some of the greatest truths of all have been confined to the smallest areas, and of all the truths which have been confined love is without doubt the most imprisoned, although it is the greatest truth of all.

You have perhaps been taught to believe that in seeking the love of another you can only expect certain crumbs because the human is incapable of complete giving of self. You have perhaps been taught that although within your heart you carry an ideal of the individual you would most like to know in intimacy, there can be no such ideal. You have been trained perhaps to believe you can only give so much, that you can only do so much and that you should do no more because then it will be the turn of others to give to you.

This is not love. There is no bargaining, there is no holding back, there is no expectation in love. It is everything in itself, so human considerations do not enter the picture. Teach this to your mind. It is the most important lesson you can give to your human brain in this lifetime or any other.

Love will last beyond—beyond the goals of your particular lifetime, beyond the expression of your particular physical body, beyond any plane in which you may exist at future dates. Love will never stop. It cannot be stopped, and in understanding this you will never again be afraid. What can you fear when you know *you* are going on forever and no other individual or thing can prevent your going on?

Love freely, but also understand this as you do: Loving freely does not consist of indiscriminate actions toward any individual who crosses your path. You can give love in the form of attitude to some individuals and they will understand and accept your attitude for what it is. With other individuals you maintain the attitude but must speak a word to them for them to understand. For each individual who comes within your atmosphere there is some expression of love you can give. Learn to realize which expression will be of most benefit to the individual you encounter and act accordingly.

Your attitude will be unchanging, your expression will be varied. This must be so because in giving love you are giving your greatest gift, and it must be accepted by the other individual for a love action to be completed. The other individual is capable of understanding love to a certain degree, and whatever his degree of understanding is it will call forth from you the proper action that he may gain in his own awareness.

You need not attempt to direct your actions, you need not attempt to direct your feelings, you need not attempt to direct any part of what you do with love. When you have trained your mind to be open to the promptings of your heart, you have only to follow in physical activity the dictates of your mind, which is transmitting the love action from within you. You do not need to think anything out. You do not need to analyze, to ponder, to study, because everything you need is ready to go into action instantly, right now.

Give love its own head. Let its beauty touch everywhere you walk, let its loveliness affect everything you touch. Let its greatness make you the great individual you are in truth. You are not a limited, unattractive, unsuccessful, unknowing individual. *You* are everything everyone else has ever been, you are all that God is if you will simply open yourself and allow that God to be all that he is, if you will open and allow love to be all that it is, for the human shell is like a radio transmitter. From the transmitter itself there comes forth no broadcast at any time. It is simply a channel *through* which the broadcast from somewhere else may be passed on to come forth as expression; and like the transmitter, your body is simply a channel through which God wishes to express in an individual manner his complete being.

This is why you cannot with intelligence make your own decisions with your human brain. This is why you cannot with success chart your own course through life with your human brain, and this is why you cannot with happiness allow others to have any part in the decisions you make about your own destiny.

You must allow love to take over, you must allow love to be the master of your physical being, of your life, if you would be happy.

Love is the colors which delight your eye, love is the sky which stands between your planet and the spaces of eternity. Love is the mountains which give their strength to the world, love is the sea which pounds upon the shore with a power so mighty it can be overwhelming. Love is the sands of the desert which warm the small animals by day, love is the stars which light the birds at night. Love is the moment between two human beings when in silence they can feel they are indeed one.

162

Love is the air you breathe, it is the ground upon which you step. Love is the food the trees and the plants produce that your body may have fuel with which to operate. Love is every expression in existence, and in the natural parts of God's material plane you will find love expressing itself fully. That you do not always understand is simply an indication that you have not reached a point of awareness which will make activity clear to you.

Seeming cruelties, seeming injustice do not exist because they cannot. There can not *be* evil, there *can* not be anything except God, therefore there cannot be anything except love. In any plane of existence, in any condition, in any activity, in any expression there can only be love.

So, open yourself to this truth. Love every part of your physical existence, not with a conscious determination that you will pretend it so you can fool God into thinking you feel love, but with the knowing that although your human mind does not understand the motives for being where you are and what you are at present the motives are based upon pure love.

Love everyone with whom you are in contact, not with a fawning air materially, not with the surface attitude that regardless of what these individuals do they are acting in pure love, but with the *understanding* that if their actions toward you are not pure love in reflection, they *are* expressing love with an unknowing activity, a distorted reflection, which will in time be changed to an undiluted channel of the great God himself, when their understanding reaches that point of acceptance.

Love without demand and love constantly. Love so you yourself may be what you are supposed to be, so that you may become everything that you long to become, so that you may experience all you are meant to experience and can therefore write a successful, triumphant finish to your earthly tasks when this lifetime has come to an end. And when that time comes, you will go forth from your physical body with love, in which there is no room for fear or hesitation. You will enter the consciousness of the next plane awaiting you with complete love, knowing love is what you are, love is what you do, love is everything you feel.

Love thy God beyond all others, because God is you, God is love, God is all things in his own being. He is the core of all that is, so love God beyond all others. Love him in the midst of your mortal misery if you have seeming misery until your understanding overcomes the attitude you have had and you realize you do *not* have misery, that all is well with you.

Love God when you must toil at hard labor, so you can reach the understanding it is *not* hard labor and it is not toil, but you are expressing in an activity, a giving for some purpose which will benefit others. When everything seems to have gone awry, love God, because in seeming distortion of events, your love will clear the way for you to see through that distortion and there will be nothing wrong.

Love the Creator for the beautiful blue of the sky and the pure whiteness of the clouds. Love your Creator for the trees reaching toward heaven, for their soft swaying and dancing. Love him for the winds that make the trees dance, for the sound of the music in the winds, for the freshness they bring. Love him for the loveliness of the flowers, for the countless colors of his nature, for the birds and their singing. Love him for everything in your life, for in love you are blessed in the midst of poverty, you are protected in the threat of danger, you are rescued from the mires of anything by your Creator.

Love, love, love. It is the key to riches beyond your knowing, it is the answer to every question, every lack, every search of the material being. Love, and you will be filled with a glow that you can feel. Love your family, your neighbors, your fellow workers, strangers who pass by. Love your self, not in egotism but in humble wonder that you too are a marvelous mechanism made by the One who created all things.

Seek to know love, and soon you will find love has discovered all of your secrets. Open yourself that love may come to you and soon you will find love was within you all the time. Love as if you would never again have the opportunity to give of self, love as if the heavens would fall any moment if you did not.

Try loving with all of your might for just one day. Perhaps you cannot maintain an attitude of compassion, of understanding for an entire day, and if you cannot then love for an hour, for half an hour, for whatever length of time you can maintain without reservation an outpouring of self completely.

Practice until the expression of love becomes you and you are indeed giving it for an entire day, for day after day. When you have reached this point, you will find you have also reached such an awareness you are no longer a creature of your earth but you are awake to the reality of all that which lies beyond.

Love, and there will be no questions, no frustrations, no failures. Love, and you are sending the Creator forth with irresistible power, you are being your true self, you are making your own way easy. Love, and time has no meaning, days hold no emptiness.

Love, and you are immortal, you are filled with the ecstasy of God's warmth, you are permeated with the glory of God's power, and you are lifted to the light of God's being.

LOVE ON THE MATERIAL PLANE

The basic expression of love is one thing and one thing only, everywhere, all the time, but the surface expressions of that basic love are so varied they are like every other part of God's material creation, beyond counting.

Very often love is expressed in the physical world in some way which causes it to be misunderstood by the human mind. The mind is not capable of understanding until it has been trained to do so, so it is not surprising that love is often ignored when it stands close by, often misinterpreted when it seeks to touch.

Surface expressions cannot be numbered or placed in categories, even though they are a part of the material world. The attempt has been made throughout the years of civilization to confine everything to some department of numbers, to some description of characteristics. But the only thing which can be fully depended upon to conform to what is expected of it is the Creator, God himself, love itself.

The *surface* expressions of his love, however, are so varied they confuse many individuals into regarding them as something other than love. Actions upon the surface, because their motives are seldom known and even less seldom understood, are accepted so often by those who receive them or observe them as entirely different to that which they truly are intended to be.

You yourself have probably misunderstood the intent of some individual in performing an act for you or to you, suspecting that individual of some ulterior motive and then learning his motive was entirely honest and loving.

It is the habit of the human mind to suspect everything everyone else does. If a beneficial action takes place, it is the habit of the material mind to seek for the profit to the one who performed the action. If a favor is given, it is the habit of the material mind to expect that the one who gave the favor will ask a favor in return at some time.

The human habit, a very distorted one, is to consider that all parts of contact with every human being upon the earth have "strings" attached to them; that if a good is done the doer will expect a good deed in return; that if a sacrifice of some kind is made, he who sacrifices will expect a sacrifice upon the part of the recipient; that business cannot be conducted with honesty and compassion; that friendship cannot be a matter of complete trust; that families cannot share with each other, because some member will claim the lion's share for himself.

It is too bad this human habit has been allowed to be maintained for so long. Throughout the history of the world as it is known at present, you can find records which will attest to the fact that this state of suspicion, mistrust, fear, hesitation, has existed since recorded civilization began. Before that time, undoubtedly, in other civilizations, the same attitude was maintained. If it had not been, people would have come to such an understanding of each other there would have been no destruction of those civilizations, as there must have been or the world would have progressed in awareness far beyond the point to which it has come to this date.

A man will express friendship for someone, and be cause the mind has been trained from childhood to be suspicious, the one to whom that gesture is made will

168

automatically draw back in suspicion as to what this man could possibly be seeking for himself.

Misunderstanding does not need to continue beyond the moment of realizing it is misunderstanding. Within each heart there beats love, within each being there is the longing for oneness. The only lack in the material world is that the mind does not *know* until it has been trained to know that these qualities are *within*, waiting to express *without*, and that expression of these qualities will join all, with no exception.

Love offers many openings in the physical world. Because it is constant and everywhere, there is always an opportunity to express love in some way, wherever you are, whatever you are doing. It is not always obvious in its expression upon the surface plane. Sometimes it is subtle, sometimes it is invisible and sometimes it is so quiet it goes completely unnoticed by anyone except the one who receives it.

Love does not need a loud hosanna for recognition. It does not need an audience to play its part. It makes itself felt and known in so many ways that it seems the human mind cannot accept the fact one quality could spread itself so far, in such variety.

The love of God speaks through each individual. The sound of his voice depends upon that individual's ability to open that it may come through. When love is suppressed, it grows and grows within until in time it explodes upon the surface. When this happens a physical action takes place which is more often misunderstood than not.

Because of suppression the action becomes a distortion of love. It is not the pure, easy-flowing action which *motive* gives to it but the ignorant, unknowing action which results from too much pressure undirected and over-controlled until it has become uncontrolled. Acts of violence result from this suppressed, mis-directed love, and are condemned by others as crime, as sin, as insanity.

If every child was trained from earliest infancy to express his love freely, there would be no such situations left upon the earth. If love was freely expressed by both male and female there would be no complexes, there would be no frustration, there would be no enmity between the sexes.

Love must be free to be true and clear. Therefore, understand that the expressions upon the surface of some things in the past which have perhaps seemed to you to be without reason result from the human habit of suppression of self.

When a man seizes a woman in unwanted violence, it is because somewhere, sometime, perhaps for a long time, he has suppressed the natural inclination in his being to give his pure, eternal love. He has suppressed the God within, due to the static in his human brain, his transmitter, which prevented his bringing forth the true message as it came from the source. When anyone does something of this nature it is for the one reason. There is no other reason than love, just as there is no other quality to existence except love.

When you have encountered one whose distorted expression was so strong you were impelled to move from his vicinity, you were reacting automatically to an instinct to remove yourself from the vicinity of distorted love. The atmosphere about that individual would be so upset, so inharmonious, your own body would feel it and would be affected by it to the extent it would move you physically from that place, or make you ill.

If you have encountered someone who has attempted to express his feelings in some manner which was not pleasing to you, do not look back upon the experience with unhappiness or with fear, should you have maintained these reactions until now. Understand he was driven beyond his control by that overwhelming urge to be at one with all things in love, for it is present within each one and cannot be ignored, set aside, since it *is* that of which each one consists. This individual may have performed some act which is termed criminal, but he was driven by his deepest need, his pure intent, to express love. His lack of awareness distorted the expression of his perfect motive.

If a man has been educated, trained to be a lawyer and suddenly he is faced with the task of building a house, he is not condemned or criticized because he is not prepared by education and training to build that house. If it is necessary for his family to live under other arrangements for some time, arrangements less comfortable, until he contacts someone who *is* qualified to build his home for him, he is not criticized because his family must be inconvenienced.

Yet, if a man is not educated to understand the things which are within him, if he is not trained to express his inner being in a balanced, happy way on the surface, he is treated as if he were something less than human, as if he were less than the earth beneath the feet of those who condemn him. He is not given time or opportunity to find the self who can build his undistorted physical expression for him, he is not allowed to inconvenience

171

the comfort of his fellow beings while he awakens to truth. Instead, he is regarded as something not worth saving, as an object for destruction or confinement or, at the very least, ostracism.

The mind is educated in school. It is trained along certain lines, and an individual is not expected to follow other lines than those in which he was trained. The study of the creative truth, of the basic being, is almost completely ignored and then, when the inevitable reaction to unknowingness sets in, the human mind condemns its own impulses, truth-based though they are.

In the previous chapter, love was described in its purest form. The ideal attitude of any individual was discussed. You were told to love everything, everybody, everywhere. Now turn to the surface, or what most people consider the "practical" side of this expression.

It is all very well for someone who does not know your circumstances, who is not familiar with your experiences, to say to you, "Love, love, love. Love by day and by night. Love everyone without exception. Love indiscriminately in your attitude, though not in your actions. Love constantly, with every part of your being."

This is truth, but it cannot convey to your human mind suggestions as to *how* you shall express that love with your material being, and if you are untrained, unpracticed, untaught, unknowing in this, you will be at a loss as to exactly what you should do. It is not enough to say to you that there is no necessity for your deciding a course of action, once you allow love to take over your life.

It is true that the actions of your surface being in expressing love, once you have accepted the allness of it, the rightness of it and the truth of it, will be simple if you have trained your physical self to be subjective to the directions of your inner being. Since most individuals are very thoroughly untrained, however, for the moment approach this matter with the attitude that your material being, though eager and willing, is unpracticed in the habit of complete obedience to self. Therefore, your human person will need instructions from your true being for every step it is to take in beginning to express God's love. It will need to know how to start moving, and then it will need to know what it should do once it does move. Until it is accustomed to operating as it was meant to operate, the mind requires detailed instructions from your eternal intelligence.

You begin moving, becoming active as a love-being, by accepting the truth. This is your beginning, this is the start. All love needs, all your sweet being needs, is *recognition* to institute movement in the proper direction. Just as you acknowledge an acquaintance by recognition of him, so you accept the existence of truth by recognizing it, by giving it attention.

You do not need to make some conscious, material gesture in order to begin. You have already begun when you accept that love is the basic element from which everything was created. If it is strong in your mind, you are ready to use this acceptance you have, to live with it.

Now you have begun, what shall you do next? Like any part of whatever you strive to accomplish, you begin in small ways that you may build through the habit of *doing,* that you may encourage your mind by the more easy accomplishments in the beginning, that you may make the foundation for the shining temple of love you will become consciously before you are through with your life span.

What are small ways? They are small only in material relationship to other material ways in which you can express later. Nothing is small or unimportant in reality, but certain phrases must be used in approaching the human mind, which is accustomed to certain phrases and must be spoken to in its own language until it can learn the language of truth.

Therefore, you begin in small ways to express your love. If you serve other individuals in some capacity, you will show that love you have accepted by an unfailing courtesy, by an *attitude* of wishing to serve, by an enthusiasm for continuing to serve as long as you can be of use. You will not become impatient with those who are impatient toward you. You will not become disgusted with those who do not seem to know what they want. You will not become weary of giving your smile, your attention.

This may seem small indeed, but if you are one who serves, you know that as a human being it has not been easy in the past for you to maintain such an attitude, to follow such a pattern of action. It is the human inclination to respond in like to that which is offered from others in the way of attitude, of words, of deeds, and it is not anything less than a herculean task for the surface being who is unawakened to give only that which he would like to receive instead of that which he does receive.

You do not know how far your kindliness, your courtesy, your friendliness will spread, because when you touch one individual with it that individual carries it to the next individual he encounters, and so it goes without end until it has traveled beyond your plane, beyond your universe, and continues in the endless reaches of creation until it comes back to you. Once such an action has been instituted, it never again comes to a standstill and it returns to you, it is renewed within you and passes through, strengthened, expanded, on its way again for the benefit of someone else.

If you are one who is served by others, you have an even greater opportunity for expressing love because you are in a position to create a certain situation, whereas if you must serve, those you serve create the physical situation. Perhaps you are waited upon sometimes with less than full efficiency, with less than complete enthusiasm. You will find that if you are a considerate individual, if you express gratitude for every part of the service given to you, the service itself will improve in every way.

You may pay for these services with coins, but you are not giving what you are receiving if that is the only way you give. Genuine gratitude for that which others do to wait on you is the coin with which they should be paid also. Their surface beings must earn money with which to maintain their persons, but the inner beings must have from your inner being a recognition of the love they are giving by serving, a response to that which they offer you in order for them to be completely satisfied with their work, happy to be working for you.

Give your attention to your attitude in contact with those who are not socially connected with you, whether they are in authority over you materially or you are in authority over them. Watch yourself and observe whether you have been in the past a giver rather than a grasper.

This alone will insure growth swiftly in your ability to express love upon the surface plane.

You have opportunity every day to give expression to your love. In some manner you contact others whether it is directly, by telephone, by correspondence, or by thought. You are in contact with someone, somewhere, every day. When you speak a word to another, be sure that word is kindly. When you perform an action which involves another individual, be sure that action is without ulterior motive, completely honest, and only for the purpose of accomplishing a happy result.

In any relationship in your world, if you will apply the attitude that what you say is said with a loving for that one to whom you are speaking, if you will act with the attitude that what you are doing is an act of recognition of the God-self in both of you, you will grow. If you will not judge the words and actions of others, you will be expressing love toward all. The world is full of criticism today. It can well spare one critic, and you who are aware of what you are, of the wonderful potentials in expressing that greatness upon the surface, can surely resign from the ranks of the ignorant at once.

It is not easy for the human mind to relinquish the habit of allowing words to leap into your mouth when the action of some individual is contrary to what your brain thinks it should be, or is foreign to your understanding of human behavior. A constant watch upon your tongue for a time will soon bring you the reward of speaking kindly to everyone, thereby gaining an effortless habit of kindliness.

Happiness is the inevitable result of expressing the best that is within you, and happiness draws others to you so they may bask in its light. You become more and more at one with the world for which your surface person was created, you become more and more one with the individuals with whom you were created, and you become more and more that which you long to be above and beyond the misery of your self-criticizing, fault-finding customs of the past.

Yes, love is a practical thing, it is *not* a namby-pamby thing. It is not fawning or servile at any time, under any circumstances. It is not possible for love to do other than love, so the admonition Jesus taught of turning the other cheek was not a teaching to be meek. It was only to make clear to those who were ready to understand that in love you turn the other cheek because there is no reason to do otherwise.

You do not turn the other cheek offering it to a belligerent one that he may strike you again, physically, vocally, or in any way, but so you may not show the cheek which was struck, to remind him of something of which he would have to be ashamed.

The strongest individuals are those who express love regardless of what other individuals may be expressing, and in the material world this is strength indeed! They have the control *by* self to maintain their attitudes constantly and they have the activity of the Eternal Intelligence which impresses upon their minds the truth that they are responsible for what they do, not for what anyone else does; that what they feel within is the reality, and any deviation in their expressions without would not be real at all. Wanting to be real they are practical, and being practical, they continue to express their true beings.

You can do it as surely as anyone could ever do it. The

master teachers did it, master ones are doing it now upon your earth, and you too can accomplish constant expression of self if you only want to do so, for in that self you are also a master.

In loving expression upon the surface, there is no need under any circumstances for you to lie down that someone else may wipe his muddy feet upon your clothing. There is no need at any time for you to offer yourself as a whipping post to someone who wishes to vent his anger. Your duty to your self in the love way is to *understand* that the one who would wipe his muddy feet upon you only wishes to do so because he is afraid that if he does not you might trample upon him. The one who wishes to use you for a whipping post only does so because he feels he himself should be whipped and will not give in to that self-castigating condemnation.

Understanding, upon the surface, consists of controlling the human inclinations in your mind toward distortion, any of the emotions, the non-existing emotions with which human beings live side by side yet miles apart, year after year, throughout their lifetimes.

When you can look upon your neighbor who gossips unceasingly and understand that neighbor talks only because there is no understanding of the great interests within with which he could occupy himself, you have attained love.

When you can speak to the belligerent with calmness, with friendliness, despite words which would cause the unknowing to go into battle, you have found the way of expressing love.

When you can erase any inclination within your mind to strike someone for something that individual has said or done to displease you, you have found the way to love him.

When you can *control* distorted emotion you have taken a step, but beyond that, when you can *understand* and therefore do not yourself have distorted emotion, you have reached the peak of your attempts to express love on the physical plane.

In your material world, since it is so individual, no listing can be given to you of specific acts of love you may perform, for your need of expression is not the same as that of anyone else. You can only take general examples, you can only take suggestions, and apply these to your individual physical expression in your own individual manner. Has it not been said many times that nothing can be blueprinted for you in the material dimension, but only suggested?

You live with the rest of your world, regardless of your position, regardless of your location, regardless of your age, your race or your religion, and you have every opportunity to find some expression upon the material plane for love.

If you have not been one to demonstrate in a physical action how you feel, you have perhaps criticized yourself for this lack of expression and may have gained a reputation for being what others call cold or unfeeling. Since the deepest part of love is within you, it is not necessary for you to wish to touch others with your hands, to bestow a kiss upon someone else, or to put your arms around another. This is simply one type of material expression for the inner motive, and it is only necessary to those who have a compulsion to perform such actions. If you are the kind of person who gives love by your attitude and nothing more, you are fulfilling your own destiny. You have an individual method of expression upon the surface plane. Follow this individuality in love as in everything else you do as a material being.

You may find a means of expressing by helping those who cannot seem to help themselves, not necessarily by giving of coin or supply but by giving of the attitude that here is a fellow being with whom you would share your love, to whom you would give your encouragement, and toward whom you would exhibit understanding; that this is not an inferior being because of any material circumstances; that this is not an individual to write off the record book of humanity due to circumstances which are not considered ideal in your world.

If you would give expression to your love in the physical world, all you need do is make yourself a controlled, constant transmitter of the love which will express itself at every opportunity. If this does not seem like a practical suggestion to you, give it a chance to show you how easy it becomes to let love into your life.

The first person you encounter after you have read these words can be the object of your experiment so you may prove to your physical mind that love expresses easily, that love does not require complicated activity, long hours of practice to be made known. Whatever your contact, whatever the circumstances, this is all you need to do to prove beyond doubt to your mind that love requires no training, that it is the mind itself which requires the teaching and the practice.

Maintain in your physical consciousness the truth that vou are God expressing love and that you are love expressing God. Maintain in your conscious mind every moment you are with this individual that you have a bond which joins you together—unbreakable, unchangeable—, which makes you identical. Maintain in your conscious mind the fact that the surface characteristics of that individual are no more his being than your surface characteristics are *you.* They are an expression of his self, and like your own, sometimes distorted.

Maintain in your conscious mind that you are with God, and you will find if you do this with honesty, if you truly do it, you are regarding this individual with new reverence, you are listening to what he has to say with respect, you are accepting what he is doing with understanding and you are experiencing with him a harmony, a balance which will be so wonderful you will be reluctant to break the connection between you to go on about your affairs.

This action cannot fail if you will only remember to keep your mind occupied with the recognition of divinity which you have and which this other individual has, if you will keep your mind occupied with the fact that love is everything there is in any place. It does not matter if your mind rebels, it does not matter if your mind tries to refuse acceptance. If you will simply keep it *occupied* with this truth it will be filled with it to the exclusion of all else, and the purposes of your experiment can be carried forth.

This will prove to the static transmitter, the "doubting Thomas," which is an untrained mind, that love indeed has all intelligence within itself, knows exactly what to do and when to do it, and that if you will practice the relaxation of your human mind until it truly becomes dormant beneath the control of your eternal intelligence, you will be a master in the world of men.

You will be so much there will be no room for any-thing except your realization that love fills the world and has only to be recognized, that love *is* within every part of the physical plane and has only to be given awareness to take control of your life, of every part of your world, of every part of your planet.

Upon the surface it is actually very simple to express love because essentially, in the final conclusion, the *expression* of love is just to give that which you would like to receive. This, the Golden Rule, is the most practical, the most usable, the most successful law you could ever hope to live by, you could ever hope to express with.

Give your love by giving courtesy, consideration, compassion. The words may sound difficult, but once you start using that which they indicate you will find they are very easy indeed. You are a superior being because you are a supreme being, as everything else in creation is superior and supreme, so it is no problem at all for you to become what you already are. You have only to discover what you are.

Since your material being is an expression God has created for his own use, your surface self is as great as your inner self. Its seeming lack of greatness has been due only to your mental lack of recognition for that greatness, your transmitting machine's not being directed and controlled. *Recognize* everything you are, all that you are, and you will *be* all that you are.

Love given in the material world in its purest form is so complete in itself there can be no room for any of the ideas of the human mind to impose themselves. The pure giving of self is expressed by many means through the physical vehicle in the physical dimension, however, for each individual must express love to be complete and each being in an individual position, must have a varying way of expression. It is the same love, it moves from the same motive, but it is brought forth upon the surface with variation.

If the repeating of this truth still has not made it too clear to your physical mind, approach it from this direction: God is expressing himself, or itself, through all parts of the world you can understand with your material intelligence; through people, through animals, through plants, through water and air, through minerals. Love is God, therefore love is expressing itself through all of these material things. The human attention has not been given often to this truth, so the human understanding of it is small.

For instance, the mineral kingdom of your world is little understood beyond those scientific offerings of explanation as to the chemical contents, their monetary value and the purposes for which they may be used. Little thought, if any, has been given to the fact that since God caused *everything* to express, there must be love in *all parts* of the physical world, not just in the more animated ones with which people are familiar.

It is not necessary for you to know the exact expressions of your world, but for happiness and peace it is necessary that you understand each thing *is* expressing love, and that by giving your love you will receive that which is being expressed.

Each individual thing contributes some variation of the love which is God. There is no difference in its extent, there is no difference in its quality, there is no difference in its power; but so love would reach the material consciousness of everything on the physical plane, God has varied himself.

It is obvious that the physical characteristics of the different expressions vary greatly, but there are two basic facts which apply to everything. One is the beforementioned individuality of every expression regardless of its category. No two human beings are identical, no two doves are identical, no two trees are identical, no two rocks are identical. Second is the truth that each thing has a beauty of its own which, when observed, can be fully appreciated and when fully appreciated, draws forth that feeling of oneness, of identification with whatever is under observation.

Each thing you do or say with a conscious attention of love is a part of your eternal progress toward oneness. It does not matter if you step aside to save crushing an insect in a garden, or if you give service to a human being. It does not matter if you give your admiration to the flowers growing along a path, or if you refrain from trapping and killing an animal. It does not matter if you contemplate water and lose yourself in its mystery, or listen to words from someone for whom you care. None of these things matter in themselves in the sense that one is more important than another, or that one means more than another. Whatever you give in love is fully as important as any expression in the material world.

The man who sacrifices his physical being for his country does not make a more magnanimous gesture than you do if you speak with love to someone who could call forth your impatience.

184

The man who gives service to humanity does not give love more truly than you do when you feel a real identification with a living creature who is not one of your own physical kind.

Understand this clearly: That *any* expression of undiluted, undistorted love is important, fully as important, as any other expression. The smallest attention to pure love is as full as the most complete, as the largest. The smallest part of God is exactly the same as the greatest part of God, since he is both, since he is all.

Pure love *can* be expressed between material individuals, and it does not matter what their positions are in relation to each other. It does not matter whether they are of the same race, of the same social level, of the same age, because pure love *is not* that which it has seemed to be to the human mind. Love in itself requires no physical action. Love in itself *is*. It is expressed through *attitude*, and the material understanding takes it for expression as its limited conception of love can express.

Remember, *you are love*, and you are attempting to express that love-self through your physical lifetime. Remember, it is the surface unawakening to this truth which causes distress in your human self. It is the material lack of awareness which causes you to be suppressed, to transmit incorrectly the motives for your existence.

If your mind has not grasped the meaning of the words written regarding reality and that which is not real, perhaps understanding will come by this means.

It was stated before that there cannot be such things as hate, fear, envy, greed, any emotions which are termed negative, since all is love. You may have wondered how it can be that these do not exist when you have felt them yourself. Any confusion here is due to your not realizing that your material being *thinks* it experiences and convinces itself that it does, while your eternal self *knows* what is real and what is not.

If, in your younger days, you were ever alone at night and heard a noise with which you were unfamiliar, you can probably remember the terror which gripped you and the things your mind pictured. You went through a terrible experience waiting for some menace to descend upon you, thinking this one moment was going on forever. When you learned the cause of the noise you found there was nothing to fear whatsoever, there was no danger, and only seconds or moments had passed. But during those moments your fear, your terror, the danger, the eternity were as real to you as if they had actually existed.

Perhaps this explains to you why emotions can seem to be real when they are not, when they do *not* exist. You cannot actually have any experience which is called negative, because God is the only *reality* in existence and God is totally love.

When something is total, all, there could hardly be anything else. You can misunderstand love, you can *think* it is something else, and your physical being, accepting the distorted reflection of fact, will respond with a manufactured emotion. This *does not* make the emotion real; it only *seems* to be real.

When you were a child, you no doubt played in a world of make-believe, as children will. When you gave your complete attention to your make-believe, it became reality to you while you maintained that absorption.

Once you have learned to immediately release any distortion so you are aware at once of truth within you and about you, you will have rid yourself of misery in any of its many forms invented by the human mind so it may torture itself.

Love cannot be comprehended by the mind which has been schooled only in hatred, in envy, in selfishness, until that mind is awakened to the truth that it is operating only because love causes it to operate; that it could not exist if love did not wish it to exist; and that it has no power whatsoever except that which is fed to it by love.

You can begin taking steps toward the light of understanding by telling your mind until it *must* accept that you are equally love, that all things are equally love, and that God alone knows exactly how everything should express that love without disturbance. You can then work side by side with everything else in existence for the glorification of the Eternal Intelligence.

Working side by side you will come to a love for everything, and by loving everything you will freely allow it to find its own destiny as you are finding yours. You will fit harmoniously with all other parts of your world, every one of which was created to operate in perfect harmony with every other one.

You will find your inner knowing has come through into your surface awareness and is expressing materially the truth that *love is all.*

RESUMÉ

You have been told that love is endless and eternal. For this reason it cannot be confined, so love which is offered to you must be accepted gratefully, without any effort to imprison it if you are to realize the full happiness it brings to you.

Love must be free and can only be free, freely given. Since it is essentially everything, it would be like attempting to harness a star or to force the moon to another course to tell love where it shall express, to what degree, and when it may express itself.

The individual who has the privilege of receiving the undiluted, unselfish love of another cannot help feeling the expanding glory within which is his response to that love, unless he is so busy blinding himself to truth he does not see the great and priceless gift he is receiving.

Where can you find anything upon the material plane which compares to the treasure love is? When you give thought to its actual quality, what it means to you and to everyone in the world, you will realize it is incomparable, unmatchable.

God is constant and unchanging, so there is no change in the constancy of love. The degree of love must be due to the individual ability to express it. The awareness upon the surface plane of love must be due to the individual understanding of its coming. Love itself cannot be anything except what it is.

You are nothing else except what you are. In your true being, the deathless self, you are unchanging because *you* are God. The changes, the variations in you as an in-

dividual and in all other individual expressions are due
only to the degree of consciousness with which you express on a material level.

You cannot die in any way, *you* cannot cease to exist,
because *you* have always been. You can express by some
physical means for only a few material years before you
go on to further activity elsewhere, or you may express
for hundreds of years physically before you go on to other
things elsewhere. But the *you* which is expressing cannot
be less than it was before time began, than it will be
after all necessity for physical expression has ceased.

You truly are completely love, since you are completely
God, all that is. Your mind may rebel against accepting
this fact, because the human amnesia, the forgetfulness
of being self, causes the mind to enjoy wallowing in its
own misery, its belief in a temporary existence and no
more. Self-pity is a favorite emotion upon the human
plane, among human beings, but like every other distortion of love it is simply an unawakened response to the
love of *self* which is expressing within your deepest being, where there is no ego or self-indulgence of any kind.

Self-pity, self-indulgence, self-consciousness, self-criticism are not terms which refer to your *self*. They refer to
your *surface* being, the *reflection* of you, and each should
be one word, not two, to be correct—selfpity, selfindul-
gence, selfconsciousness, selfcriticism. They cannot apply to *you,* since you are perfect in all ways at all times.

Self-pity, feeling sorry for yourself, is a surface activity, a surface emotion, which is a false reflection of
the fact that your self loves your surface being, just as
God loves any part of the surface world, and in that love
has compassion for surface ignorance of truth. There is

no room for tears in your eyes at the suffering upon the surface of others or of yourself, because these sufferings are *seeming* realities only. The true beings do not suffer, and once these moments of seeming suffering are past, they have made no mark in the records of eternity because they did not exist in the first place.

It is not easy for the human mind to understand this truth because of its training in an almost totally opposite direction, which teaches that the human being is unhappy if it *thinks* it is, that it is miserable if it *thinks* it is surrounded by misery, that it is any of the things which are termed unhappy if it *thinks* it is any of these things.

But how can one positive, radiant, powerful, eternal, constant, all-encompassing, beautiful thing produce anything which is totally opposite to itself? Since all parts of creation are intelligent and without error, the answer to that question is that it cannot produce anything except its like, except its identical like.

If you are color blind, you will look at one color and see it as another, but that color remains what it is nevertheless. It is your awareness which is distorted, although it seems real to you until you reach an understanding of the fact that the color is not what you see it to be, but in reality is its true shade. Apply this to any distortion of truth, to anything which detracts from the clear picture of love, to anything which changes the true expression of love, to anything which makes you seem to be less than or other than what you are.

When you look into a mirror you see your reflection, but it is not a true, undistorted picture of your surface being because it is opposite to yourself. Your right side is your left side in the mirror, your left side is your right, and so it is with the physical reflection of the true being. When you *reflect* your self, fact is distorted. It only *seems* to be that which is apparent upon the surface and in reality is not that seeming expression at all. When you are *being* your self, you are expressing the true purpose for which you were individualized.

Love comes to you whether you are conscious of it or not. It works around you constantly when you are awake. It protects you constantly as you sleep. If there are any unpleasant experiences your surface being seems to go through, it is because the understanding of your human mind has distorted truth until that mind has drawn to you some experience which is *not* a true expression of love.

You are not to be criticized for this. You are simply being alerted to the truth that if you are unaware, unawakened in your conscious being, your physical self, you are liable, open, to experiences which will make you misunderstand even more the basic causes for your existence, the reason for your expression, the motive for your actions.

Love is so much it fills you to overflowing in any moment you make a direct contact with it, if it is only for a second, for an hour or a year. Time is not an element for consideration beyond your daily schedule of activity, so you can live an eternity of exaltation in one moment of pure love, as fully as you live an eternity of exaltation in years of pure love. In moments of distorted fear, or of any strong emotions, you have felt you were experiencing an eternity. This is because time is only applicable to your clocks and your calendars, to your consciousness of it. It can stand still or it can move at an incredible rate of speed, in proportion to that which you experience in your mind. A dream can last one second in time by your clock, and yet in your awareness it can have gone on for hours or even days.

Learn to recognize time for what it is and apply it in your understanding of love. In the past you may have thought that a momentary expression of love by one word of recognition or courtesy to another was unimportant. If you will realize time's place in your expression and put it in that place, you will no longer regard it with any degree of awe, with any degree of recognition as your master.

You can say one word with pure intent and start actions which will change your life beyond your wildest dreams, just as effectively as you can spend hours pouring forth kindliness and reaping the same harvest. It is not the amount of time you give, it is not the number of individuals you contact. It is your *intentional* expression of *pure feeling* which produces action. It is your love expressed without any defilement, detraction, which reaches into the atmosphere for results.

When you have expressed one moment of pure love, you have touched the place where the angels stand waiting to receive you in their midst. When you have expressed one purely unselfish, giving action, although it is but a small gesture upon the part of your physical person, you have given back to God that which he gives to you. You are expressing God, your self, toward others as God expresses toward you through other things.

You have only to learn control *by self* of your physical being to become a love-light which will attract the attention of every knowing thing in existence, of which there are awarenesses beyond counting. If you do not at this moment understand the importance of that statement, you will in time realize that the more other awarenesses recognize you for what you are, the more fully you are able to express that which you are in the eternal spaces of creation and therefore bring through into your surface world the beauty, the joy, the greatness, all of which are attributes of God.

The human race, for the most part, misunderstands the true greatness of its Creator, and each expression of that greatness helps to draw forth into the light for all to see what God really is. Each expression helps to erase the false impression of a God who exists as but half a ruler with an individual who rules the other half of Creation in the name of evil. It erases the impression of a God who can do nothing or will do nothing unless he is coaxed, bribed, deceived or approached in a certain way. It erases the impression of a God who is only a man of whim, of emotion, and it erases the impression of a God who is anything except love.

Your love is what you need to express beyond your physical need to breathe, to eat for sustenance and to drink to quench your thirst. It is your greatest need.

You may have felt the lack of almost everything in the material world and have suddenly found an expression of love so fulfilling you not only no longer require material comforts but have no interest in them whatsoever.

Your atmosphere upon the surface plane has no importance at all in relation to your eternal being except that this is where you express your self, through your physical vehicle. What you express is entirely up to your individual mind, because there you transmit the love which is making itself impressed, as it impresses upon every mind in creation. Every individual thing is receiving the urging motive of love for everything that expresses. There is no other impression made by the Eternal Intelligence, there is no other action taking place anywhere in reality. Love is the only thing that happens to you, love is the only thing you can do, love is the only thing you will ever find in your present plane, or in any dimension beyond your present world.

What seems to be other things is not possible. Remember this and grow in strength until your physical being can no longer be affected by this mis-understanding, or lack of understanding, which other individuals might attempt to impress upon you. Gain in awareness of this fact that you may not mistakenly believe with your human mind that you have encountered anything except love.

When you can know truthfully, when you are aware in every part of you, material as well as eternal, that this love is everywhere and everything, you will have such a protection you will notice no harm comes to you in any manner. You will have such a shield of love about you you will notice no resentment or malice of any kind is sent in your direction with deep intent, as deep as the human mind can make it.

When you have gained a constant awareness of love. you have gained all there is in your world. Once you have reached that one moment of complete realization of love which is inevitable as long as you are humbly, sincerely seeking to realize it, you will know why love cannot be interfered with, why it cannot be ignored.

Love truly fills every pore in your physical body once

that body is made aware of love in its undiluted strength. Once love fills your mind in its pure truth you will know there is no room for anything else while that love is expressing. In this way your human expression understands the true facts about love, why it is that love can be gentle without being weak, why love can triumph against the strongest hatred, why love can fulfill in the midst of material misery, why love can replace any material loss, why love can be seen wherever the eye turns, why it can be heard wherever the ear listens, why it can be felt wherever two things of creation come close to each other. In your moments of silence, as awareness grows within your mind of the truths which are not taught to you in educational schools, the hugeness of love's truth will be proved beyond any doubt for you.

If you should attempt to explain in words to anyone else what you have realized for yourself, remember that in the past you could not understand the full impact of the truth of love, no matter how many words were used to present it to you, in what manner it was given to you. Remember that it was necessary for your physical being to *experience* the fullness of love undiluted, to *feel* it, before your mind could understand what others have understood only when they too experienced it for themselves.

Remember that words can only encourage you to find your own awakening to the glory that is love, and you will not attempt to explain what you have experienced, you will know that you would only be wasting your effort. You can help others toward their own awakenings to love once you have found yours by your attitude, and if they ask of you the source of your happiness you can, if you wish, tell them that you have realized love is the one reality in existence. If they cannot accept this, they cannot accept anything else you might say by way of an attempted explanation.

The only thing the words in any part of this book can do for you is to convey a very small part of the feeling with which they were produced. The words can only give you a hint of love, the oneness with which they are written for you, personally and especially. The words can only offer you a statement which in itself has no meaning until, through your experiencing the feeling behind the words, you can understand the meaning itself.

But there are no strangers, friend. There are no aliens, no enemies. There are no lessers or greaters. There is just oneness from which everything became individualized expression upon material planes. There is only oneness which does not change, which does not falter, which goes unrecognized by those who have not awakened from their long sleep, unknowing, not aware, without consciousness of *self*.

You can speak words of love which are completely empty if they are only words, and you can say nothing and convey great love because you are feeling it. When you can feel that love which is carried upon the magnetic current throughout your atmosphere, when you can feel in your surface self that love which is your basic being, then and only then will you understand, will you *know*, the reason these words were given for you to read, then and only then can you understand the motive with which this book was written.

The desire to serve is the most basic urge in the being of anyone who is aware of the love pulsating through and permeating that individual's existence, within and without. There is no other thought which comes into the human mind of an individual who is aware of love other than the desire to give in some manner to the rest of creation. There is no urging upon others to follow the promptings of the individual who expresses love, there is no longing for human power, there is no desire for human recognition. There is nothing except the overwhelming, the spilling-over love which *must* be expressed through the physical being in the ways open for expression, because the material body cannot contain this glorious feeling indefinitely without expression.

You have just as strong a desire to express love as anyone, anything, anywhere. If you have not been conscious of this desire before, give it your attention now, for it is there, and although you may try to ignore it you cannot. It is too strong, it is *you*. It is your very existence, here and beyond here.

If you have had resentment because you are lonely or unfulfilled and have tried to express that resentment in your attitude toward others, you will lose these distorted emotions, which are not real but are synthetic, as you accept consciousness that love must take first place in your desires, in your wants, in any part of your expression in your world. Be honest with yourself, be honest in your mind that you may open it to the honesty of truth, and you will soon cease to be anything less than happy, serene, joyous, constantly active in some manner with the expression of the love pouring forth from the fount which never runs dry, which is without limit.

You may have clung in the past to resentments and because of habit your mind can be reluctant to let these resentments go, but *you* are much stronger than your physical mind in every part of its expression, so *you* by your love can cause relinquishment of resentment. It may not be instantaneous, but it *can be*, for you are what you are regardless of what you have thought you were, and you can express what *you* are regardless of what your mind may have thought you were expressing in the past.

You can cause your mind to relinquish fear of others, you can cause it to relinquish reluctance to move through life with courage, with daring. You can cause your mind to accept, not with a force which would be recognizable to the surface world as a belligerent overwhelming, but through a force which allows the overwhelming love-power to fill it. In filling your mind with love you do not leave room for anything else. You do not need to worry that in giving kindness, consideration, love to others, they will retaliate by deeds, words, actions which will hurt you. When you attain true expression of love they cannot hurt you in any way.

If a cup is full it has no room for more, and so if you are full of love no distortion can enter your physical being. You are already love itself; remember this, so you have only to fill your surface self with that love to be a *complete* expression of God.

The surface being is God in expression and the surface being of everything else in creation is God in expression. The true you is the God which expresses. The surface and the eternal are the same thing, but the one *is* God, the other is the reflection of God, the expression of God, the activity of God, as a singer is his voice and a recording is the expression of that voice. Both are parts of the same thing, but one is the original, the other is the reflection of the original. Your eternal self is being what it is, your surface self is expressing what you, the eternal, are. When you reach the full awareness which enables your surface being to express at all times exactly what you are, you will have completed your journey toward that constant, true beingness with God.

Love is so many things they cannot all be expressed were you to spend your lifetime discoursing upon this one subject. Even with words, which are limited, you would not run out of things to say about love. Truth cannot be changed. It can only be repeated, so all parts of love which are described, discussed, or thought of in the physical world are the many varying facets of the one fact: the changeless, eternal glory of God.

How long can anyone go on explaining this most vital, fascinating subject? He could go on forever, without end. What you have read is not even one drop in the ocean of love, in proportion to its truth, to its actual size, to its capacity, to what it is capable of accomplishing, to what it is.

But if you will accept even this small part of the overwhelming majesty of love it will be enough to transform your physical life. One small part of love can change the course of your world. One small part of love can change every part of your physical expression, including your body, your mind, and the attitudes of those about you. One small part of love can make time stand in its tracks, can make space nothing. One small part of love can do anything, without a limit, because in that small part is contained everything that love is in its entirety. Since love is endless, nothing and no one could ever express all of love. This is why the expression of even a little bit of it accomplishes so much.

What have been called miracles are easy for those who can use an aware activity of love. What you need most in order to accomplish what you are here to accomplish is just one part of the love you are in truth, so give your attention to that magnificence and ignore the petty small-nesses created only in the world of materiality to occupy the human mind, created by the human mind, expressing in misery anywhere it touches—misery which is not real, but seems to be because it is accepted as real.

Just as an individual who professes to be something he is not is accepted by others as that which he professes to be rather than what he is until he is exposed, so the dis-tortion of love has been accepted upon your planet as a real condition, as real activity, because the truth has not been given attention, has not been exposed to the light of awareness.

You will see when you give attention to the truth it will be made known to you that it is true. When you give attention to love you will be filled with it. When you give attention to knowing that this is God, your life will be filled with God to the exclusion of eveything else.

Others who are not aware, of course, will still be at-tempting to express according to their understandings, but they will not be able to pass their ignorance into your atmosphere, into your life, because of your knowing of truth. In your own understanding you will be able to send into their atmospheres truth which will dispel some part of their unawakened expressions and will help them to their own individual awarenesses of love.

It will amaze and delight you, as a human person, once you have activated this truth, to see the reactions to what you are doing and being. It will be like a new game you discovered as a child, which so enchanted you you had no thought for anything else. You will become so engrossed in playing this wonderful game of giving love, of expressing love, you will forget all about the grubby, everyday duties you have thought were necessary occupations for your mind. You will forget all of the worries and the cares, you will forget anything of the past in the way of resentments and failures.

You will only be conscious of the now of your existence, of the glorification of God which lifts your physical being with it so you are more than an inhabitant of your planet, so you are much more than the body and mind who used to think it was operating independently of anything beyond itself.

In love you will find delight, enchantment. You will play with it, you will use it, you will laugh with it, and you will be serious with it. Through it all will run the deep, deep joy, this high, high ecstasy that so fills the knowing ones they have no time for attempting to draw others into their understanding but are solely concerned with giving because of it, not explaining what it is. Because you can find this understanding yourself as a human being, you are going to experience that same exaltation.

You are going to find the truth that beyond your plane lie so many things which have been ignored or scoffed at, that there are so many discoveries for you to make, you will not again give attention to any limitations, to any possibility that you might cease to exist when your physical body is no longer needed.

You will find yourself in the company of the angels, producing with them the music of reverence, of worship, which automatically expresses itself from the core of any being who is aware of *what* he is.

You will put your hand upon an animal in love, when in the past you might have struck, attempted to kill its physical being. You will gaze into the heart of a flower without touching it, whereas in the past you might have plucked it and caused it to die before its time. You will worship every part of God's world consciously, seeing its true beauty because you will be looking through the eyes of love, and you will live with your fellow beings in true harmony because your material self will be existing in the awareness of truth.

You will be past any need, because you will know you have no needs. You will have a singing gratitude that God is making himself active through the body and mind you are familiar with, and you will be aware that it is true—*you* are that God expressing, although your mind may have recoiled in horror when it first met this truth, although it may have been incapable of considering this truth when it was first presented to you.

In being what you are, you cannot help being all things of God, because your mind will have no part in that action. What you are is beyond your mind, and the love expressed in so many ways upon the surface plane will in its truth be constantly expressing from the depths of you.

You will find you have no need to wait for another

lifetime, another dimension, another course of learning. There will be no ego, no misunderstanding about false importance of physical self.

Now, today, while you are still in the material world, you will find completion, fulfillment, heaven.

You will find all that you are is God, LOVE.

ALL THAT YOU ARE

How can anyone not believe in a God of some kind when there is one sunset to watch, one song to hear, one hand to touch?

The material world is itself proof of God's existence, and it is an infinitesimal fraction of the proofs offered in the spaces beyond earth atmosphere, in the dimensions other than the one you know.

If you have had doubts of the existence of any kind of Supreme Intelligence, mark your doubts as a stirring to discover truth. You may be a member of some religious denomination which does not fit your particular needs. If so, be honest enough to leave that organization and join the one which does offer you personally a certainty of God. You may be a church member who regularly attends services, who gives time and effort to church projects, but are unfulfilled despite your activities. If so, be honest enough to meet your God somewhere else, wherever you can find him.

God is a very personal thing to each individual, so do not be afraid to seek your own. He cannot be a divine man to all, nor can he be an impersonal intelligence to everyone. Individual experiences produce individual understandings of truth, and so is required any number of ideas, or ideals about God.

The one sure truth is that a God of some kind *is*. All of the atheistic explanations in your world do not provide answers to how anything came to be. How "accidental" life could begin on a planet when the planet's existence is not explained can only be a part-answer and that part unsatisfactory.

If there is no God, what is the universe? How is it there are stars and earth and people? Why does anything exist if all is nothing?

This desolate attitude is caused by an individual's own fumblings with the experiences of life. He claims there is no God because he can see no beauty, no wonder with his self-imposed blindness. His fear has turned him away from the obvious.

Equally unseeing are those who claim all unhappiness is God's fault, that whatever they are, whatever they experience, has been caused by something they could not control. These too are of the fearful, for they blame their own lack of understanding on the only One who understands them completely.

Look at the order of your universe if you would seek material proof of God. Do the planets collide, do the stars leave the sky? Do not all things follow a pattern, again and again, in mathematically perfect cycles? Look at the resources of your world if you would find proof of God. Is there not food to eat, water to drink? Does the sun not cross the heavens each day, rest each night? Look at your fellow beings if you would find material proof of God. In their best moments, do they not give their physical selves for each other? Do they not share their plenty with those who are hungry? In their best moments, do they not bind the wounds of a hurt animal?

Look to yourself if you would seek further proof. Does your body not function as other bodies do when it is in normal health condition? Does your heart not beat without your prompting, do you not breathe without conscious volition?

Everywhere there is proof of some Supreme Intelligence, some perfect Thing. Those who do not see the proof are blind because they will not see. They are dedicated to bitterness, and as long as they remain in this distorted state they will not be aware of God, of their true beings, nor will they have happiness, contentment for a moment.

You may have had stirrings of doubt, of bitterness, but did you not overcome these with your faith and go on, strengthened by the application of that faith to a distortion of the truth? You have done this, anyone can do it, because there is a God, and that God is a true expression of his own Being.

Whenever you are inclined to doubt a Creator, look about you again for proof God is indeed a reality.

When you read of the accomplishments of masters who cause seeming miracles, who can levitate themselves from one location to another instantaneously, who can supply all of their surface requirements by holding out their hands, do you wonder if your own efforts are useless? Do you think you should be able to do likewise if you are to be a true expression of God?

Then take heart and do not be discouraged. Be comforted, and do not regard yourself as a failure. In your material world, the masters who make their mighty deeds known do so to show that through use of natural laws you also can overcome any physical rule. They are giving you examples of truth in action, beacons by which you may find your way.

As a human being expressing among other human beings, you could not perform the deeds of the masters without setting yourself apart physically. When you are ready to be alone, your surface self will be completely subjugated and you will employ the natural laws which are a part of your divine self. Until that moment in your growth comes, you must understand you do not have shortcomings simply because you are still anchored to the earth. *No one has shortcomings.*

The masters can walk through fire unharmed. This you can do also when your understanding reaches the point of *knowing* nothing can harm you because all things are one with you. It is the distortion fear which brings harm to the physical body in any way.

The masters travel with the speed of thought. This you can do also when you reach the understanding that the physical laws of gravity, of distance and of time apply to the density of matter, and that creation, following the laws of eternity, is limitless, timeless, one with your eternal being.

The masters heal the sick and the injured. When your awareness of the magnetic current has developed to the degree that you are acting as a funnel for its power, you too can heal. You can do anything any other part of creation can do, not by setting your mind to its accomplishment, but by setting *aside* your mind so your real intelligence may operate.

If God had limitations the pattern of existence would be haphazard, would it not? In all of creation there is no erratic action, no chance working of the laws. Everything is ordered, in place. Here again is reason why you are in your rightful place, again reason why your intuitive directions are the way through which to express.

When you train your mind to accept this truth, it no longer attempts to lead but is content to follow.

You have been given suggestions as to how you may follow the promptings of your best self. Whether or not you choose to use them is up to you. You have been told you can find your own way if you will stop being fearful so your true being can indicate your perfect pattern.

No one can *make* you change your habits. No one can change them for you, no one can offer anything except encouragement. If you have been depending on someone else for your salvation, wake up now and realize the truth. Another can help you to begin your journey by giving you a strong hand to hold until your feet are firm on the path. He cannot take the journey for you.

If you have been depending on printed studies for your knowledge, stir yourself now and realize you will educate your mind in the world's way of reasoning but you will not find eternal wisdom in books, or hear it from the teachers who quote them.

Whether you have many years yet to live or most of them are behind you, whether you are lacking in worldly experience or have had many material activities, you can achieve a oneness with God *now*. The truth is yours at any age, at any stage of your education, at any hour of day or night. It will never be offered for sale because it is priceless. It will never be given in words because it is beyond description.

Even with the purest of motives, even with the most loving of attitudes, no one can give you truth itself. It must be experienced, realized, *felt* by you or you cannot grasp it. No one can describe personal experiences so they become yours. You can only recognize them, understand them when you have experienced their like.

Recognition of truth comes *from* the inner self to the outer self, so all the words, all the instructions, all the encouragement you can find will be useless if you yourself do not realize what truth is.

It is the deepest desire of those who serve to give you understanding of the reasons behind your actions. It is the most humble wish of the aware to convey to you a fraction of the love which is yours regardless of surface appearances. Accept, then, any sincere words for what they are—mortal attempts to join in oneness consciously with that which is already one in truth.

Any writing is inspired by the Supreme Intelligence, any painting is inspired by Divine Beauty, any music is inspired by the Eternal Harmony of Creation. The intent is pure, loving and completely selfless. The expression is less only because it is confined to the abilities of the surface being. You are the solemn responsibility of all other beings, of the writer, the artist, the composer. If you are not happy they have failed you, but if they are not happy you have failed them, for they are your responsibility also.

Your world is divided against itself because it has lost the trust, the faith in its Creator, because it has insisted all parts share a common misery instead of a common understanding. Your individual world must be set to rights before any part of your earth can be balanced, because just one person's lack of understanding will keep your planet out of line. All things contribute to the larger thing. If you will balance your life with awareness, your world balances by one more degree. If you wait for someone else to do it, you will wait a long time and will eventually find someone else is waiting for you to do it.

Suffering is not confined to the individual manifesting it materially. It carries on the atmosphere to everything else of your world, to you. Ease your own suffering, therefore, and you lighten the sufferings of others. Ease the sufferings of others, and you lighten your own.

You are your own world and you are of the worlds of all others. You are the light in the darkness about you, or you are the darkness about the lights of others. Take the responsibility which is yours, of reflecting physically the wonderful being *you* are. Accept this responsibility and live so you are expressing your part in creation, for this is your task alone and none can perform it except you.

You are so great in your true being it staggers the human imagination, and so limited in past expressions of that greatness you have been unaware of your eternal self. If this were not true you would not pick up a book to read, you would seek no suggestions to follow. You would consciously have awareness of self, and this is completion.

All you need is yours to use now. All you will ever accomplish is yours to accomplish now. All you are ever going to be you can be now. *You are* God, *you have* God, *you do* God. You have only to accept this with your human mind to release the marvelous *you*.

All that you are is God, all that you are is Creation itself, all that you are is *everything*. This is a truth by which to live here, now, and in the nows of other dimensions, with love totally directing your life.

Remember, dearest one, all that the earth is you are. Remember, most beloved, all that you are is all there is.